The Treasury of Christian Poetry

The Treasury of Christian Poetry

Compiled by Lorraine Eitel,
With Jeannine Bohlmeyer, Lynn M. Fauth, Gerald W. Healy,
Daniel Taylor, and Christian Weintz

Fleming H. Revell Company
Old Tappan, New Jersey

"Lord, Hear My Prayer," by John Clare, used courtesy of Routledge and Kegan Paul, Ltd.

"The Bridegroom of Cana" and "Resurgam" by Marjorie Pickthall reprinted by permission of The Canadian Publishers, McClelland and Stewart Limited, Toronto.

Quotations from *The Psalm of Christ*, by Chad Walsh, Westminster Press, 1963. By permission of the author.

"The Gardener to His God" from Mona Van Duyn, *A Time of Bees* (Copyright © 1964 by Mona Van Duyn) in *Merciful Disguises* (Copyright © 1973 by Mona Van Duyn) Reprinted with the permission of Atheneum Publishers.

"The Choice of the Cross," from THE DEVIL TO PAY, by Dorothy Sayers. Copyright 1939 Dorothy L. Sayers, renewed 1966.

"Ecce Puer" from THE PORTABLE JAMES JOYCE. Copyright 1946, 1947 by The Viking Press, Inc. Copyright renewed © 1974, 1975 by The Viking Press, Inc.

"The Creation" from GOD'S TROMBONES by James Weldon Johnson. Copyright 1927 by The Viking Press, Inc. Copyright renewed © 1955 by Grace Nail Johnson.

"Pax" from THE COMPLETE POEMS OF D. H. LAWRENCE Copyright 1933 by Frieda Lawrence. Copyright © 1964, 1971 by Angelo Ravagali and C. M. Weekly, Executors of the Estate of Frieda Lawrence Ravagali.

"Morning Glory" from COLLECTED POEMS by Siegfried Sassoon. Copyright 1918, 1920 by E. P. Dutton & Co. Reprinted by permission of Viking Penguin Inc.

"Noah's Prayer" from PRAYERS FROM THE ARK by Carmen Bernos de Gastold. Translated by Rumer Godden. English text copyright © 1962 by Rumer Godden. Reprinted by permission of Viking Penguin Inc.

"How Many Heavens" reprinted from THE COLLECTED POEMS OF EDITH SITWELL by Edith Sitwell by permission of the publisher, the Vanguard Press, Inc. Copyright © 1968 by the Vanguard Press, Inc. Copyright 1949, 1953, 1954, 1959, 1962, 1963 by Dame Edith Sitwell.

"The Hurricane" is reprinted from THE COMPLETE POEMS AND SELECTED LETTERS AND PROSE OF HART CRANE, Edited by Brom Weber, with the permission of Loveright Publishing Corporation. Copyright 1933, © 1958, 1966 by Liveright Publishing Corporation.

"Carol," by Howard Nemerov, from THE COLLECTED POEMS OF HOWARD NEMEROV. The University of Chicago Press, 1977. Reprinted by permission of the author.

"Indifference" and "The Great Wager," by G. A. Studdert-Kennedy are used by permission of Hodder & Stoughton Limited.

Library of Congress Cataloging in Publication Data
Main entry under title:
The Treasury of Christian poetry.
   1. Christian poetry. I. Eitel, Lorraine
PN6110.R4T73   821'.008'0382   81-21106
ISBN O-8007-1291-9   AACR2

Contents

Introduction

The reader of a collection such as this is entitled to a statement, however brief, of the criteria for selection. Our intention is to include some of the widely known and appreciated poems of the Christian faith and, beyond that, to collect works which are not so well-known but still worthy. An important criterion was that the poems be suitable for reading aloud (as poetry was originally meant to be). The poetry in this anthology is, for the most part, explicitly Christian in outlook. Much fine poetry that rightfully can be called Christian is not explicitly so and is therefore outside the boundaries of this collection. Conversely, no claim is made that every author represented here is an avowed Christian, orthodox or otherwise. The poems have been allowed to stand by themselves as varying expressions of the Christian experience.

Foreword

The following compilation is the work of Lorraine Eitel and her colleagues in the Department of Language and Literature at Bethel College, St. Paul, Minnesota: Jeannine Bohlmeyer, Lynn M. Fauth, Gerald W. Healy, Daniel Taylor, and Christian Weintz. The idea for this anthology was generated by their students from Oral Interpretation classes, who recognized a need for poems on various Christian themes that would lend themselves to vocal interpretation as well as silent reading. Lorraine Eitel communicated that idea to us, and in the ensuing pages you will experience it. Here is a unique and comprehensive compilation that spans the literary period from the seventh century A.D. to the present. We trust it will serve you well.

THE PUBLISHERS

Maker of Heaven and Earth

THE CREATION

And God stepped out on space,
And He looked around and said:
"I'm lonely—
I'll make me a world."
And far as the eye of God could see
Darkness covered everything,
Blacker than a hundred midnights
Down in a cypress swamp.
Then God smiled,
And the light broke,
And the darkness rolled up on one side,
And the light stood shining on the other,
And God said, *"That's good!"*
Then God reached out and took the light in His
        hands,
And God rolled the light around in His hands,
Until He made the sun;
And He set that sun a-blazing in the heavens.
And the light that was left from making the sun
God gathered it up in a shining ball
And flung it against the darkness,
Spangling the night with the moon and stars.
Then down between
The darkness and the light
He hurled the world;
And God said, *That's good!*
Then God himself stepped down—
And the sun was on His right hand,
And the moon was on His left;
The stars were clustered about His head,
and the earth was under His feet.
And God walked, and where He trod
His footsteps hollowed the valleys out
And bulged the mountains up.

Then He stopped and looked and saw
That the earth was hot and barren.
So God stepped over to the edge of the world
And He spat out the seven seas—
He batted His eyes, and the lightnings flashed—
He clapped His hands, and the thunders rolled—
And the waters above the earth came down,
The cooling waters came down.

Then the green grass sprouted,
And the little red flowers blossomed,
The pine tree pointed his finger to the sky,
And the oak spread out his arms;
The lakes cuddled down in the hollows of the ground,
The rivers ran down to the sea;
And God smiled again,
And the rainbow appeared,
And curled itself around His shoulder.

Then God raised His arm and He waved His hand
Over the sea and over the land,
And He said, *Bring forth! Bring forth!*
And quicker than God could drop His hand,
Fishes and fowls
And beasts and birds
Swam the rivers and the seas,
Roamed the forests and the woods,
And split the air with their wings,
And God said, *That's good!*

Then God walked around
And God looked around
On all that He had made.
He looked at His sun,
And He looked at His moon,
And He looked at His little stars;
He looked on His world
With all its living things,
And God said, *I'm lonely still.*

Then God sat down—
On the side of a hill where He could think;
By a deep, wide river He sat down;
With His head in His hands,
God thought and thought,
Till He thought, *I'll make me a man!*

Up from the bed of the river
God scooped the clay;
And by the bank of the river
He kneeled Him down;
And there the great God Almighty,
Who lit the sun and fixed it in the sky,
Who flung the stars to the most far corner of the night,
Who rounded the earth in the middle of His hand;
This Great God,
Like a mammy bending over her baby,
Kneeled down in the dust
Toiling over a lump of clay
Till He shaped it in His own image;

Then into it He blew the breath of life,
And man became a living soul.
Amen. Amen.

JAMES WELDON JOHNSON

HYMN

Now we must praise heaven-kingdom's Guardian,
the Creator's might and his mind-plans,
the work of the Glory-Father, when he of wonders of every one,
eternal Lord, the beginning established.
He first created for men's sons
heaven as a roof, holy Creator;
then middle earth mankind's Guardian,
eternal Lord, afterwards made—
for men earth, Master almighty.

CAEDMON

14

GETTING INSIDE THE MIRACLE

No, He is too quick. We never
catch Him at it. He is there
sooner than our thought or prayer.
Searching
backward, we cannot discover *how*
or get inside the miracle.

Even if it were here and now
how would we describe the just-born trees
swimming into place at their green creation,
flowering upward in the air
with all their thin twigs quivering
in the gusts of grace? or the great
white whales fluking
through crystalline seas
like recently-inflated balloons? Who could
time the beat of the man's heart
as the woman comes close enough to fill
his newly-hollow side? Who will
diagram the gynecology
of incarnation, the trigonometry of trinity?
or chemically analyze wine
from a well? or see inside
joints as they loosen, and whole limbs
and lives? Will anyone stand beside
the moving stone? and plot the bright
trajectory of the ascension? and explain
the tongues of fire
telling both heat and light?

Enough. Refrain.
Observe a finished work. Think:
Today—another miracle—the feathered
arrows of my faith may link
God's bow and target.

LUCI SHAW

WHAT WORDS HAVE PASSED

"What words have passed thy lips, Adam severe?
Imput'st thou that to my default, or will
Of wandering, as thou call'st it, which who knows
But might as ill have happened thou being by,
Or to thyself perhaps? Hadst thou been there,
Or here th' attempt, thou couldst not have discerned
Fraud in the serpent, speaking as he spake;
No ground of enmity between us known,
Why he should mean me ill, or seek to harm.
Was I to have never parted from thy side?
As good have grown there still a lifeless rib.
Being as I am, why didst not thou, the head,
Command me absolutely not to go,
Going into such danger, as thou saidst?
Too facile then, thou didst not much gainsay,
Nay didst permit, approve, and fair dismiss.
Hadst thou been firm and fixed in thy dissent,
Neither had I transgressed, nor thou with me."
   To whom, then first incensed, Adam replied:
"Is this the love, is this the recompense
Of mine to thee, ingrateful Eve, expressed
Immutable when thou wert lost, not I,
Who might have lived and joyed immortal bliss,
Yet willingly chose rather death with thee?
And am I now upbraided, as the cause
Of thy transgressing? not enough severe,
It seems, in thy restraint! What could I more?
I warned thee, I admonished thee, foretold
The danger, and the lurking enemy
That lay in wait; beyond this had been force,
And force upon free will hath here no place.
But confidence then bore thee on, secure
Either to meet no danger, or to find
Matter of glorious trial; and perhaps
I also erred in overmuch admiring

What seemed in thee so perfect, that I thought
No evil durst attempt thee! But I rue
That error now, which is become my crime,
And thou th' accuser. Thus it shall befall
Him who, to worth in women overtrusting,
Lets her will rule; restraint she will not brook,
And left to herself, if evil thence ensue,
She first his weak indulgence will accuse."
    Thus they in mutual accusation spent
The fruitless hours, but neither self-condemning,
And of their vain contést appeared no end.

JOHN MILTON
From *Paradise Lost*, Book IX

THE LATE PASSENGER

The sky was low, the sounding rain was falling dense and dark,
And Noah's sons were standing at the window of the Ark.

The beasts were in, but Japhet said, 'I see one creature more
Belated and unmated there come knocking at the door.'

'Well let him knock,' said Ham, 'Or let him drown or learn to swim.
We're overcrowded as it is; we've got no room for him.'

'And yet it knocks, how terribly it knocks,' said Shem, 'Its feet
Are hard as horn—but oh the air that comes from it is sweet.'

'Now hush,' said Ham, 'You'll waken Dad, and once he comes to see
What's at the door, it's sure to mean more work for you and me.'

Noah's voice came roaring from the darkness down below,
'Some animal is knocking. Take it in before we go.'

Ham shouted back, and savagely he nudged the other two,
'That's only Japhet knocking down a brad-nail in his shoe.'

Said Noah, 'Boys, I hear a noise that's like a horse's hoof.'
Said Ham, 'Why, that's the dreadful rain that drums upon the roof.'

Noah tumbled up on deck and out he put his head;
His face went grey, his knees were loosed, he tore his beard and said,

17

'Look, look! It would not wait. It turns away. It takes its flight.
Fine work you've made of it, my sons, between you all to-night!

'Even if I could outrun it now, it would not turn again
—Not now. Our great discourtesy has earned its high disdain.

'Oh noble and unmated beast, my sons were all unkind;
In such a night what stable and what manger will you find?

'Oh golden hoofs, oh cataracts of mane, oh nostrils wide
With indignation! Oh the neck wave-arched, the lovely pride!

'Oh long shall be the furrows ploughed across the hearts of men
Before it comes to stable and to manger once again,

'And dark and crooked all the ways in which our race shall walk,
And shrivelled all their manhood like a flower with broken stalk,

'And all the world, oh Ham, may curse the hour when you were born;
Because of you the Ark must sail without the Unicorn.'

C. S. LEWIS

SONNET

The Bible says Sennacherib's campaign was spoiled
By angels: in Herodotus it says, by mice—
Innumerably nibbling all one night they toiled
To eat his bowstrings piecemeal as warm wind eats ice.

But muscular archangels, I suggest, employed
Seven little jaws at labour on each slender string,
And by their aid, weak masters though they be, destroyed
The smiling-lipped Assyrian, cruel-bearded king.

No stranger that omnipotence should choose to need
Small helps than great—no stranger if His action lingers
Till men have prayed, and suffers their weak prayers indeed
To move as very muscles His delaying fingers,

Who, in His longanimity and love for our
Small dignities, enfeebles, for a time, His power.

C. S. LEWIS

L'ENVOI

Now in a thought, now in a shadowed word,
Now in a voice that thrills eternity,
Ever there comes an onward phrase to me
Of some transcendent music I have heard,
No piteous thing by soft hands dulcimered,
No trumpet flash of blood-sick victory,
But a glad strain of some vast harmony
That no brief mortal touch has ever stirred.

There is no music in the world like this,
No character wherewith to set it down,
No kind of instrument to make it sing.
No kind of instrument? Ah, yes there is;
And after time and place are overthrown,
God's touch will keep the one chord quivering.

EDWIN ARLINGTON ROBINSON

RESIGNATION

O God! whose thunder shakes the sky,
  Whose eye this atom-globe surveys,
To Thee, my only rock, I fly,—
  Thy mercy in Thy justice praise.

The mystic mazes of Thy will,
  The shadows of Celestial night,
Are past the power of human skill;
  But what the Eternal acts is right.

Oh teach me, in the trying hour—
  When anguish swells the dewy tear—
To still my sorrows, own Thy power,
  Thy goodness love, Thy justice fear.

If in this bosom aught but Thee,
  Encroaching, sought a boundless sway.
Omniscience could the danger see,
  And mercy look the cause away.

Then why, my soul, dost thou complain—
  Why drooping seek the dark recess?
Shake off the melancholy chain;
  For God created all to bless.

But ah! my breast is human still;
  The rising sigh, the falling tear,
My languid vitals' feeble rill,
  The sickness of my soul declare.

But yet, with fortitude resign'd,
  I'll thank the inflictor of the blow—
Forbid the sigh, compose my mind,
  Nor let the gush of misery flow.

The gloomy mantle of the night,
  Which on my sinking spirit steals,
Will vanish at the morning light,
  Which God, my east, my sun, reveals.

THOMAS CHATTERTON

GOD'S GRANDEUR

The world is charged with the grandeur of God.
  It will flame out, like shining from shook foil;
  It gathers to a greatness, like the ooze of oil
Crushed. Why do men then now not reck his rod?
Generations have trod, have trod, have trod;
  And all is seared with trade; bleared, smeared with toil;
  And wears man's smudge and shares man's smell: the soil
Is bare now, nor can foot feel, being shod.

And for all this, nature is never spent;
  There lives the dearest freshness deep down things;
And though the last lights off the black West went
  Oh, morning, at the brown brink eastward, springs—
Because the Holy Ghost over the bent
  World broods with warm breast and with ah! bright wings.

GERARD MANLEY HOPKINS

GOD'S WORLD

O World, I cannot hold thee close enough!
  Thy winds, thy wide grey skies!
  Thy mists, that roll and rise!
Thy woods, this autumn day, that ache and sag
And all but cry with colour! That gaunt crag
To crush! To lift the lean of that black bluff!
World, World, I cannot get thee close enough!

Long have I known a glory in it all,
  But never knew I this;
  Here such a passion is
As stretcheth me apart. Lord, I do fear
Thou'st made the world too beautiful this year.
My soul is all but out of me,—let fall
No burning leaf; prithee, let no bird call.

EDNA ST. VINCENT MILLAY

SPRING

Nothing is so beautiful as spring—
   When weeds, in wheels, shoot long and lovely and lush;
   Thrush's eggs look little low heavens, and thrush
Through the echoing timber does so rinse and wring
The ear, it strikes like lightnings to hear him sing;
   The glassy peartree leaves and blooms, they brush
   The descending blue; that blue is all in a rush
With richness; the racing lambs too have fair their fling.

What is all this juice and all this joy?
   A strain of the earth's sweet being in the beginning
In Eden garden.—Have, get, before it cloy,
   Before it cloud, Christ, lord, and sour with sinning,
Innocent mind and Mayday in girl and boy,
   Most, O maid's child, thy choice and worthy the winning.

GERARD MANLEY HOPKINS

I THANK YOU GOD

i thank you God for this most amazing
day:for the leaping greenly spirits of trees
and a blue true dream of sky; and for everything
which is natural which is infinite which is yes

(i who have died am alive again today,
and this is the sun's birthday;this is the birth
day of life and of love and wings:and of the gay
great happening illimitably earth)

how should tasting touching hearing seeing
breathing any—lifted from the no
of all nothing—human merely being
doubt unimaginable You?

(now the ears of my ears awake and
now the eyes of my eyes are opened)

E. E. CUMMINGS

22

PIPPA'S SONG

The year's at the spring
And day's at the morn;
Morning's at seven;
The hillside's dew-pearled;

The lark's on the wing;
The snail's on the thorn;
God's in his heaven—
All's right with the world!

ROBERT BROWNING
from "Pippa Passes"

A PRAYER IN SPRING

Oh, give us pleasure in the flowers to-day;
And give us not to think so far away
As the uncertain harvest; keep us here
All simply in the springing of the year.

Oh, give us pleasure in the orchard white,
Like nothing else by day, like ghosts by night;
And make us happy in the happy bees,
The swarm dilating round the perfect trees.

And make us happy in the darting bird
That suddenly above the bees is heard,
The meteor that thrusts in with needle bill,
And off a blossom in mid air stands still.

For this is love and nothing else is love,
The which it is reserved for God above
To sanctify to what far ends He will,
But which it only needs that we fulfill.

ROBERT FROST

HOW MANY HEAVENS . . .

The emeralds are singing on the grasses,
And in the trees the bells of the long cold are ringing—
My blood seems changed to emeralds like the spears
Of grass beneath the earth piercing and singing.

The flame of the first blade
Is an angel piercing through the earth to sing
'God is everything!
The grass within the grass, the angel in the angel, flame
Within the flame, and He is the green shade that came
To be the heart of shade.'

The grey-beard angel of the stone,
Who has grown wise with age, cried, 'Not alone
Am I within my silence—God is the stone in the still stone, the
                      silence laid
In the heart of silence' . . . then, above the glade,

The yellow straws of light,
Whereof the sun has built his nest, cry 'Bright
Is the world, the yellow straw
My brother—God is the straw within the straw:—All
                    things are Light.'

He is the sea of ripeness and the sweet apple's emerald lore.
So you, my flame of grass, my root of the world from which all spring
                    shall grow,
O you, my hawthorn bough of the stars, now leaning low
Through the day, for your flowers to kiss my lips, shall know
He is the core of the heart of love, and He, beyond labouring seas, our
                    ultimate shore.

EDITH SITWELL

24

From FOOTNOTE TO THE LORD'S PRAYER

I. Which Art in Heaven

Heaven which art in Heaven Our Father in Heaven,
in our hunger, in our thirst, in our darkness, in our light,
in the riches of our poverty, in the poverty of riches,
in the leaf falling, in the sap rising, in our winter
and our spring, when the earthquake shakes the mountain,
when the calm is laid upon our shoulders, in the ashes
of our sorrow, in our peace and in our terror,
Hallowed be Thy name.

> Thy name be hallowed
> morning, noon and night,
> in the quiet pulse of darkness,
> in the harpstrings of the light,
> in the wisdom of old women
> in which tart is mixed with sweet,
> in walkers walking early
> on young feathered feet.

> Hallowed be Thy name
> in the folding of the hands,
> in the plastic strength of patience
> that long waiting lends,
> in swift outgoings
> to a distant country,
> in slow returnings
> to a rooted piety;

> Thy name be hallowed
> in the tall poise of the great,
> in the comic solemnity
> of the grasshopper's gait,
> in the moment that trembles
> a molecule of joy,
> in the Grand Canyon hour
> of soul's immensity;

Thy name be hallowed
in the working of our minds,
in the action of the Spirit,
in the building of our hands,
in the speaking of our tongues,
in the using of our shame
for the kneeling and the serving—
Hallowed be Thy name.

II. For Thine Is the Kingdom

All things move in it,
the mountain that stands,
the seed that burgeons,
marked by Thy hand,
the voice of the waters,
the silence of the stone,
fruit in clusters,
the polished bone
that tides have finished,
declare Thy name.

All things passing
back to the eye,
clouds in procession
on an ever sky,
the ghost of the apple
shining through its skin,
sun in a ripple
on a bent piece of tin,
all look out
to Thy face looking in.

What is forever cannot be lost,
the Kingdom, the Power, the Glory, Thine, God of Hosts.

Though the ear is stopped to what it once heard,
the cymbals of passion around lovers' beds,
the dance band's brass heaven, the martinis in crowds
cannot quite kill the memory of the single small Voice.
In those who see and in those who are blind,
forever it moves and watches its chance;
in the hands that make, in the hands that break,
is gathered the Power that one day will strike
the temples hands build to all other gods,
and save like the stars all big and small lights
for children who wander alone in the night,
the dream of Thy beauty in their poor, fuddled heads.

What is forever cannot be lost;
pluck out the eye, Thy Kingdom stands,
give the body to the carrion crows,
Thy Power fashions the triumph of the rose;
deny Thy Glory, Thy Glory burns
in the place of tombs, in the narrowest room.
Come home, my soul, to God who waits,
listen to His word, look on His face.
In the ages of Thy wisdom let us hide our eyes,
in what has been forever let us become,
for Thine is the Kingdom and the Power and the Glory. Amen.

KAY SMITH

SILENCE, AN ELOQUENT APPLAUSE

A piece of art, a scene, a poem
Each morsel savored in silence

The echo of Handel's Messiah
Ringing unspeakable joy within

The skillful actor bowing low
A spellbound audience registers
approval

When urgent prayer's answer
comes
Tears mirror a grateful heart.

A child's hard victory is won
Parent's outstretched arms of
approbation

The miracle of a transformed life
Quiet communion soaring heaven-
ward

Empathy between two friends
A handclasp and words unspoken

In stillness glimmers such beauty
Be still and know that I am God.

LEONA GREGORY

HYMN

Framer of the earth and sky,
  Ruler of the day and night,
With a glad variety
  Tempering all, and making light;

Gleams upon our dark path
    flinging,
  Cutting short each night begun.
Hark! for chanticleer is singing,
  Hark! he chides the lingering
    sun.

And the morning star replies
  And lets loose the imprisoned
    day;
And the godless bandit flies
  From his haunt and from his
    prey.

Shrill it sounds; the storm relenting
  Soothes the weary seaman's ears;
Once it wrought a great repenting
  In that flood of Peter's tears.

Rouse we; let the blithesome cry
  Of that bird our hearts awaken,
Chide the slumberers as they lie,
  And arrest the sin o'ertaken.

Hope and health are in his strain
  To the fearful and the ailing;
Murder sheathes his blade profane;
  Faith revives when faith was
    failing.

AMBROSE OF MILAN

THE HURRICANE

Lo, Lord, Thou ridest!
Lord, Lord, Thy swifting heart

Naught stayeth, naught now bideth
But's smithereened apart!

Ay! Scripture flee'th stone!
Milk-bright, Thy chisel wind

Rescindeth flesh from bone
To quivering whittlings thinned—

Swept—whistling straw! Battered,
Lord, e'en boulders now out-leap

Rock sockets, levin-lathered!
Nor, Lord, may worm out-deep

Thy drum's gambade, its plunge
    abscond!
Lord God, while summits crashing

Whip sea-kelp screaming on blond,
Sky-seethe, high heaven dashing—

Thou ridest to the door, Lord!
Thou bidest wall nor floor, Lord!

HART CRANE

HOLY SONNET 12

Why are we by all creatures waited on?
Why do the prodigal elements supply
Life and food to me, being more pure than I,
Simple, and further from corruption?
Why brook'st thou, ignorant horse, subjection?
Why dost thou, bull and boar, so sillily
Dissemble weakness, and by one man's stroke die,
Whose whole kind you might swallow and feed upon?
Weaker I am, woe is me, and worse than you,
You have not sinn'd, nor need be timorous.
But wonder at a greater wonder, for to us
Created nature doth these things subdue,
But their Creator, whom sin, nor nature tied,
For us, His creatures, and His foes, hath died.

JOHN DONNE

RECONCILIATION

I begin through the grass once again to be bound to the Lord;
   I can see, through a face that has faded, the face full of rest
Of the earth, of the mother, my heart with her heart in accord,
   As I lie 'mid the cool green tresses that mantle her breast.
I begin with the grass once again to be bound to the Lord.

By the hand of a child I am led to the throne of the King
   For a touch that now fevers me not is forgotten and far,
And His infinite sceptred hands that sway us can bring
   Me in dreams from the laugh of a child to the song of a star.
On the laugh of a child I am borne to the joy of the King.

G. W. RUSSELL

THE SONG OF HANNAH
I Samuel 2

My heart doth in the Lord rejoice, that living Lord of might,
Which doth his servant's horn exalt, in all his peoples' sight.
I will rejoice in their despite, which erst have me abhorred,
Because that my salvation dependeth on the Lord.
None is so holy as the Lord, besides thee none there are:
With our God there is not God that may himself compare.
See that no more presumptuously, you neither boast nor vaunt,
Nor yet unseemly speak such things, so proud and arrogant.
For why? the counsel of the Lord, in depth cannot be sought,
Our enterprises and our acts by him to pass are brought.
The bow is broke, the mighty ones subverted are at length,
And they which weak and feeble were increased are in strength.
They that were full and had great store, with labor buy their bread,
And they which hungry were and poor, with plenty now are fed.
So that the womb which barren was hath many children borne,
And she which store of children had is left now all forlorn.
The Lord doth kill and make alive; his judgments all are just;
He throweth down into the grave and raiseth from the dust.
The Lord doth make both rich and poor; he all our thought doth try.
He bringeth low and ere again, exalteth up on high.
He raiseth up the simple soul, whom men pursued with hate,
To mighty ones, in chair of princely state.
For why? the pillars of the earth, he placed with his hand,
Whose might strength doth still support, the weight of all the land.
He will preserve his Saints likewise; the wicked men at length
He will confound: let no man seem to glory in his strength.
The enemies of God the Lord shall be destroyed all.
From heaven he shall thunder send that on their heads shall fall.
The mighty Lord shall judge the world and give his power alone
Unto the King, and shall exalt his own anointed one.

MICHAEL DRAYTON

POVERTY

As in the house I sat
Alone and desolate,
No creature but the fire and I
The chimney and the stool, I lift mine eye
Up to the wall,
And in the silent hall
Saw nothing mine
But some few cups and dishes shine,
The table and the wooden stools
Where people used to dine;
A painted cloth there was,
Wherein some ancient story wrought
A little entertained my thought
Which light discovered through the glass.

I wondered much to see
That all my wealth should be
Confined in such a little room,
Yet hope for more I scarcely durst presume.
It grieved me sore
That such a scanty store
Should be my all;
For I forgot my ease and health,
Nor did I think of hands or eyes,
Nor soul nor body prize;
I neither thought the sun,
Nor moon, nor stars, nor people, mine,
Though they did round about me shine;
And therefore was I quite undone.

Some greater things, I thought,
Must needs for me be wrought,
Which till my pleased mind could see,
I ever should lament my poverty.
I fain would have
Whatever Bounty gave,
Nor could there be
Without, or love or Deity.
For, should not He be infinite
Whose hand created me?
Ten thousand absent things
Did vex my poor and absent mind,
Which, till I be no longer blind,
Let me not see the King of Kings.

His love must surely be
Rich, infinite, and free;
Nor can He be thought a God
Of grace and power, that fills not His abode,
His holy court,
In kind and liberal sort;
Joys and pleasures,
Plenty of jewels, goods, and treasures
(To enrich the poor, cheer the forlorn)
His palace must adorn,
And given all to me.
For till His works my wealth became,
No love or peace did me enflame;
But now I have a Deity.

THOMAS TRAHERNE

THAT THOU ART NOWHERE TO BE FOUND

That thou art nowhere to be found, agree
Wise men, whose eyes are but for surfaces;
Men with eyes opened by the second birth,
To whom the seen, husk of the unseen is,
Descry thee soul of everything on earth.
Who know thy ends, thy means and motions see;
Eyes made for glory soon discover thee.

GEORGE MACDONALD
From *Diary of an Old Soul*

THE SCRIBE

What lovely things
  Thy hand hath made:
The smooth-plumed bird
  In its emerald shade,
The seed of the grass,
  The speck of stone
Which the wayfaring ant
  Stirs—and hastes on!

Though I should sit
  By some tarn in thy hills,
Using its ink
  As the spirit wills
To write of Earth's wonders,
  Its live, willed things,

Flit would the ages
  On soundless wings
Ere unto Z
  My pen drew nigh;
Leviathan told,
  And the honey-fly:
And still would remain
  My wit to try—
My worn reeds broken,
  The dark tarn dry,
All words forgotten—
  Thou, Lord, and I.

WALTER DE LA MARE

SHALL THE DEAD PRAISE THEE?

I cannot praise Thee. By his instrument
   The master sits, and moves nor foot nor hand;
For see the organ pipes, this, that way bent,
   Leaning, o'erthrown, like wheat-stalks tempest fanned!

I well could praise Thee for a flower, a dove,
   But not for Life that is not life in me;
Not for a being that is less than Love—
   A barren shoal half lifted from a sea.

Unto a land where no wind bloweth ships
   Thy Wind one day will blow me to my own:
Rather I'd kiss no more their loving lips
   Than carry them a heart so poor and prone.

I bless Thee, Father, Thou art what Thou art,
   That Thou dost know Thyself what Thou dost know—
A perfect, simple, tender, rhythmic heart,
   Beating its blood to all in bounteous flow.

And I can bless Thee too for every smart,
   For every disappointment, ache, and fear;
For every hook Thou fixest in my heart,
   For every burning cord that draws me near.

But prayer these wake, not song. Thyself I crave.
   Come Thou, or all Thy gifts away I fling.
Thou silent, I am but an empty grave:
   Think to me, Father, and I am a king!

My organ pipes will then stand up awake,
   Their life soar, as from smoldering wood the blaze;
And swift contending harmonies shall shake
   Thy windows with a storm of jubilant praise.

GEORGE MACDONALD

IF THOU INDEED DERIVE THY LIGHT
FROM HEAVEN

If thou indeed derive thy light from Heaven,
Then, to the measure of that heaven-born light,
Shine, Poet! in thy place, and be content:—
The stars pre-eminent in magnitude,
And they that from the zenith dart their beams,
(Visible though they be to half the earth,
Though half a sphere be conscious of their
        brightness)
Are yet of no diviner origin,
No purer essence, than the one that burns,
Like an untended watch-fire, on the ridge
Of some dark mountain; or than those which seem
Humbly to hang, like twinkling winter lamps,
Among the branches of the leafless trees;
All are the undying offspring of one Sire:
Then, to the measure of the light vouchsafed,
Shine, Poet! in thy place, and be content.

WILLIAM WORDSWORTH

God's Only Son, Our Lord

HIS THRONE IS WITH THE OUTCAST

I followed where they led,
  And in a hovel rude,
With naught to fence the weather from his head
  The King I sought for meekly stood;
A naked hungry child
  Clung round his gracious knee,
And a poor hunted slave looked up and smiled
  To bless the smile that set him free;
New miracles I saw his presence do,
  No more I knew the hovel bare and poor,
The gathered chips into a woodpile grew
  The broken morsel swelled to goodly store.
I knelt and wept: my Christ no more I seek.
His throne is with the outcast and the weak.

                       JAMES RUSSELL LOWELL

THE CARPENTER

This He was then—
A workman among working men.

He knew the orchards of Gennesaret;
The circled vineyards that were set
Like living cinctures, branch and root,
And jeweled with their purple fruit.
The somber olives, wide of limb,
Had sheltered Him
At noontide, when He had to pass
Beneath a sky of shimmering brass.
He knew the almond trees, that spread
Frail rosy clouds above His head;

The groves of oak and terebinth,
And where the fruit of colocynth
Ran tangled through the scarlet fires
Of lilies and anemones,
And where, above the walnut trees,
The tall firs lifted pointed spires.

He knew the miracle of night; the throbbing gold
Of eastern stars, merging in wistful rose
Of day, that lingers here as though to hold
The blended glories, and reluctant, goes
Down the wide hills at last, and toward the sea.
These things He knew, and all the majesty
Of planets set on height ascending height—
Vistas and terraces of light,
As though divided by a single breath,
Were God—and Nazareth.

Here were no dark misgivings, and no doubt.
All night He lived a greater prayer than words,
Until the dawn He saw the fishing-fleets go out
Like a low flight of birds.
He watched the hillslopes lightly sprayed with gold;
The olives etched in radiance, that were dark.
He saw the sheep come bleating from the fold,
And in the air, a lark.
While down the road, between the hills at last,
With tinkling bells, a train of camels passed.
With rhythmic steps, He saw them go
Upon their way to Jericho,
And in His shop, He knew, were good,
Red cedar boards and olive wood,
Where waiting for His fingers, were
The labors of a carpenter.

A night of stars and God—and then
A workman's toil with working men.

MARY BRENT WHITESIDE

THE YOUNG WORKMAN

Yes, I believe He loved them, too,
  The sons of saw and plane,
And the rhythmic ring of hammers;
  Perhaps they called again
From out the Nazareth workshop,
  Where once He used to be,
As He sat or walked with
      fisher-folk
  And gazed on Galilee.
Perhaps for loads of timber,
  Not souls, His young arms
      yearned,
For labor that, accomplished,
  Was accepted and not spurned.

Perhaps the love of building
  Grasped His hands, that folded
      lay
Or gently gestured as He talked
  About the Living Way—
Grasped them, made them fairly
      tingle
  With the energy to build,
Until the house not made with
      hands
  His earthly longings stilled.
Just as Galilean waves and fears
  Were quiet when He willed.
O Thou, our Master Builder,
  In our grime and sweat and soil
Let us ever honor Thee as Thou
  Didst ever honor toil.

MARY DILLINGHAM FREAR

THE BRIDEGROOM OF CANA

"There was a marriage in Cana of Galilee ... And both
Jesus was called and His disciples, to the marriage."

Veil thine eyes, O beloved, my spouse,
Turn them away,
Lest in their light my life withdrawn
Dies as a star, as a star in the day,
As a dream in the dawn.

Slenderly hang the olive leaves
Sighing apart;
The rose-and-silver doves in the eaves
With a murmur of music bind our house.
Honey and wine in thy words are stored,
Thy lips are bright as the edge of a sword
That hath found my heart,
That hath found my heart.

Sweet, I have waked from a dream of thee,—
And of Him:
He who came when the songs were done.
From the net of thy smiles my heart went free
And the golden lure of thy love grew dim.
I turned to them asking, "Who is He,
Royal and sad, who comes to the feast
And sits Him down in the place of the least?"
And they said, "He is Jesus, the carpenter's son."

Hear how my harp on a single string
Murmurs of love.
Down in the fields the thrushes sing
And the lark is lost in the light above,
Lost in the infinite, glowing whole,
As I in thy soul,
As I in thy soul.

Love, I am fain for thy glowing grace
As the pool for the star, as the rain for the rill:
Turn to me, trust to me, mirror me
As the star in the pool, as the cloud in the sea.
Love, I looked awhile in His face
And was still.

The shaft of the dawn strikes clear and sharp;
Hush, my harp.
Hush, my harp, for the day is begun,
And the lifting, shimmering flight of the swallow
Breaks in a curve on the brink of morn,
Over the sycamores, over the corn.
Cling to me, cleave to me, prison me
As the mote in the flame, as the shell in the sea,
For the winds of the dawn say, "Follow, follow
Jesus Bar-Joseph, the carpenter's son."

MARJORIE PICKTHALL

DESPISED AND REJECTED

Homeless!
The Living Bread
Hungered
While all beside were fed.
To their warm holes the foxes ran,
Birds flew to nest when the west
    was red,
But the Son of Man
Had not where to lay His head,

Open Door
Henceforth for all
Hungers,
Hearth and Banquet Hall
For hurt and loneliness is He
Thrust from Nazareth to
    roam,
Vagabond of Galilee,
Who is every outcast's
    Home.

KATHERINE LEE BATES

IRONY OF GOD

In vain
They shook their garments;
He did not hear the tinkling
Of little bells
On priestly hems;
Nor smell the smoky savor
Of slaughtered, burning life.

He did not see Jerusalem—
Nor Rome;
He passed by all "best families"
To dwell at last in Nazareth,
With Mary,
Mother of that Son
Who fraternized with fishermen;
Found heaven in little children;
And had a friend
Named Mary Magdalene.

EVA WARNER

THE HURT OF LOVE

O the hurt, the hurt, and the hurt of love!
    Wherever the sun shines, the waters go.
It hurts the snowdrop, it hurts the dove,
    God on His throne, and man below.

But sun would not shine, nor waters go,
    Snowdrop tremble, nor fair dove moan,
God be on high, nor man below,
    But for love—for the love with its hurt alone.

Thou knowest, O Saviour, its hurt and its sorrows,
    Didst rescue its joy by the might of thy pain:
Lord of all yesterdays, days, and to-morrows,
    Help us love on in the hope of thy gain:

Hurt as it may, love on, love forever;
    Love for love's sake, like the Father above,
But for whose brave-hearted Son we had never
    Known the sweet hurt of the sorrowful love.

GEORGE MACDONALD

WISDOM

The true faith discovered was
When painted panel, statuary,
Glass-mosaic, window-glass,
Amended what was told awry
By some peasant gospeller;
Swept the sawdust from the floor
Of that working-carpenter.
Miracle had its playtime where
In damask clothed and on a seat
Chryselephantine, cedar-boarded,
His majestic Mother sat
Stitching at a purple hoarded
That He might be nobly breeched
In starry towers of Babylon
Noah's freshet never reached.
King Abundance got Him on
Innocence; and Wisdom He.
That cognomen sounded best
Considering what wild infancy
Drove horror from His Mother's
breast.

WILLIAM BUTLER YEATS

CAROL

Now is the world withdrawn all
In silence and night
To beweeping Adam's fall
That this biography began
Of vile man.

Now the serpent smiles on sin
In silence and night
And sees the tumor swell within—
The heavy fruit that was the heart
Beat apart.

The spider's spittle weaves the
    shroud
In silence and night
Wide enough for all the proud;
Gapes the grave in pompous black
At our back.

Christ the King is born again
In silence and night
Bringing mercy to all men
Whose separate pride full is
    beguiled
By this child.

From Eden's Tree the Cross is made
In silence and night
Where Adam's bondman now is
    nailed
While the wild multitude
Cries for blood.

The great grave stone is rolled away
In silence and night
And He arose on the third day
That Adam might, free of the
    chains,
Choose his pains

And follow Him upon the Cross
In silence and night
And disdain all worldly loss
And to the compassionate King
Pray and Sing.

Therefore do we cross this hour
In silence and night
Our grief and joy, weakness and
    power,
Whereto Christ's glory and His pain
Both constrain.

For there was born in Bethlehem
In silence and night
The world's and heaven's single
    stem
That to both kingdoms we might
    then
Say Amen.

HOWARD NEMEROV

BREAD OF HEAVEN, ON THEE WE FEED

Bread of heaven, on Thee we feed,
For Thy Flesh is meat indeed;
Ever may our souls be fed
With this true and living Bread;
Day by day with strength supplied
Through the life of Him Who died.

Vine of heaven! Thy Blood supplies
This blest cup of Sacrifice;
Lord, Thy Wounds our healing give,
To Thy Cross we look and live:
Jesu! may we ever be
Grafted, rooted, built in Thee. Amen.

JOSIAH CONDER

THE LAMB

Little Lamb, who made thee?
Dost thou know who made thee?
Gave thee life & bid thee feed,
By the stream & o'er the mead;
Gave thee clothing of delight,
Softest clothing wooly bright;
Gave thee such a tender voice,
Making all the vales rejoice!
Little Lamb who made thee?
Dost thou know who made thee?

Little Lamb I'll tell thee,
Little Lamb I'll tell thee!
He is calléd by thy name,
For he calls himself a Lamb:
He is meek & he is mild,
He became a little child:
I a child & thou a lamb,
We are calléd by his name.
Little Lamb God bless thee.
Little Lamb God bless thee.

WILLIAM BLAKE

CHRIST AND THE PAGAN

I had no God but these,
The sacerdotal trees,
And they uplifted me.
"I hung upon a Tree."

The sun and moon I saw,
And reverential awe
Subdued me day and night,
"I am the perfect light."

Within a lifeless stone—
All other gods unknown—
I sought Divinity.
"The Corner-Stone am I."

For sacrificial feast
I slaughtered man and beast,
Red recompense to gain.
"So I, a Lamb, was slain."

"Yea, such My hungering Grace
That whereso'er My face
Is hidden, none may grope
Beyond eternal Hope."

JOHN BANISTER TABB

STRONG SON OF GOD

Strong son of God, immortal Love,
    Whom we, that have not seen thy face,
    By faith, and faith alone, embrace,
Believing where we cannot prove;

Thine are these orbs of light and shade;
    Thou madest Life in man and brute;
    Thou madest Death; and lo, thy foot
Is on the skull which thou hast made.

Thou wilt not leave us in the dust:
    Thou madest man, he knows not why,
    He thinks he was not made to die;
And thou hast made him: thou are just.

Thou seemest human and divine,
    The highest, holiest manhood, thou.
    Our wills are ours, we know not how;
Our wills are ours, to make them thine.

ALFRED, LORD TENNYSON
From *In Memoriam A. H. H.*

THE LANTERN OUT OF DOORS

Sometimes a lantern moves along the night,
That interests our eyes. And who goes there?
I think; where from and bound, I wonder, where,
With, all down darkness wide, his wading light?

Men go by me whom either beauty bright
In mould or mind or what not else makes rare:
They rain against our much-thick and marsh air
Rich beams, till death or distance buys them quite.

Death or distance soon consumes them: wind
What most I may eye after, be in at the end
I cannot, and out of sight is out of mind.

Christ minds: Christ's interest, what to avow or amend
There, éyes them, heart wánts, care haúnts, foot fóllows kínd,
Their ránsom, théir rescue, ánd first, fást, last friénd.

GERARD MANLEY HOPKINS

HOLY SONNET 15

Wilt thou love God, as He thee? then digest,
My soul, this wholesome meditation,
How God the Spirit, by Angels waited on
In heaven, doth make His temple in thy breast.
The Father having begot a Son most bless'd,
And still begetting (for he ne'er begun)
Hath deign'd to choose thee by adoption,
Coheir to his glory, and Sabbath's endless rest.
And as a robb'd man, which by search doth find
His stol'n stuff sold, must lose or buy it again:
The Son of glory came down, and was slain,
Us whom He had made, and Satan stol'n, to unbind.
'Twas much, that man was made like God before,
But, that God should be made like man, much more.

JOHN DONNE

THE THREE ENEMIES

The Flesh
"Sweet, thou art pale."
             "More pale to see,
Christ hung upon the cruel tree
And bore His Father's wrath for me."

"Sweet, thou art sad."
             "Beneath a rod
More heavy, Christ for my sake trod
The winepress of the wrath of God."

"Sweet, thou art weary."
             "Not so Christ;
Whose mighty love of me sufficed
For Strength, Salvation, Eucharist."

"Sweet, thou art footsore."
             "If I bleed,
His feet have bled; yea in my need
His Heart once bled for mine indeed."

The World
"Sweet, thou art young."
             "So He was young
Who for my sake in silence hung
Upon the Cross with Passion wrung."

"Look, thou art fair."
             "He was more fair
Than men, Who deigned for me to wear
A visage marred beyond compare."

"And thou hast riches."
             "Daily bread.
All else is His: Who, living, dead,
For me lacked where to lay His Head.

"And life is sweet."

"It was not so
To Him, Whose Cup did overflow
With mine unutterable woe."

The   Devil
"Thou drinkest deep."

"When Christ would sup
He drained the dregs from out my cup:
So how should I be lifted up?"

"Thou shalt win Glory."

"In the skies,
Lord Jesus, cover up mine eyes
Lest they should look on vanities."

"Thou shalt have knowledge."

"Helpless dust!
In Thee, O Lord, I put my trust:
Answer Thou for me, Wise and Just."

"And Might."—

"Get thee behind me. Lord,
Who has redeemed and not abhorred
My soul, oh keep it by Thy Word."

CHRISTINA ROSSETTI

Born of the Virgin Mary

BEFORE THE PALING OF THE STARS

Before the paling of the stars,
  Before the winter morn,
Before the earliest cockcrow,
  Jesus Christ was born:
Born in a stable,
  Cradled in a manger,
In the world his hands had made
  Born a stranger.

Priest and king lay fast asleep
  In Jerusalem,
Young and old lay fast asleep
  In crowded Bethlehem;

Saint and Angel, ox and ass,
  Kept a watch together
Before the Christmas daybreak
  In the winter weather.

Jesus on his mother's breast
  In the stable cold,
Spotless Lamb of God was he,
  Shepherd of the fold:
Let us kneel with Mary maid,
  With Joseph bent and hoary,
With Saint and Angel, ox and ass,
  To hail the King of Glory.

CHRISTINA ROSSETTI

JOSEPH'S SUSPICION

And the angel, taking some pains, told
Considerately the man who clenched his fists:
"But can't you see in her robe's every fold
That she is cool as the Lord's morning mists?"

But the other murmured, looking sinister:
"What is it that has wrought this change in her?"
Then cried the angel to him: "Carpenter,
Can't you see yet that God is acting here?"

"Because you plane the planks, of your pride could
You really make the Lord God answerable,
Who unpretentiously from the same wood
Makes the leaves burst forth, the young buds swell?"

He understood that. And then as he raised
His frightened glance toward the angel who
Had gone away . . . slowly the man drew
Off his heavy cap. Then in song he praised.

RAINER MARIA RILKE

ANNUNCIATION

Salvation to all that will is nigh,
That All, which always is All everywhere,
Which cannot sin, and yet all sins must bear,
Which cannot die, yet cannot choose but die,
Lo, faithful Virgin, yields Himself to lie
In prison, in thy womb; and though He there
Can take no sin, nor thou give, yet He will wear
Taken from thence, flesh, which death's force may try.
Ere by the spheres time was created, thou
Wast in his mind, who is thy son, and brother,
Whom thou conceiv'st, conceiv'd; yea thou art now
Thy Maker's maker, and thy Father's mother;
Thou hast light in dark; and shutt'st in little room,
Immensity cloistered in thy dear womb.

JOHN DONNE

ADVENT

Fertile and rank and rich the coastal rains
Walked on the stiffened weeds and made them bend;
And stunned November chokes the cottonwood creeks
For Autumn's end.

And the hour of Advent draws on the small-eyed seeds
That spilled in the pentecostal drought from the fallen cup:
Swept in the riddled summer-shrunken earth;
Now the eyes look up.

Faintly they glint, they glimmer; they try to see;
They pick at the crust; they touch at the wasted rind.
Winter will pinch them back but now they know,
And will not stay blind.

And all Creation will gather its glory up
Out of the clouded winter-frigid womb;
And the sudden Eye will swell with the gift of sight,
And split the tomb.

BROTHER ANTONINUS

I HAVE LIGHTED THE CANDLES, MARY

I have lighted the candles, Mary . . .
How softly breathes your little Son

My wife has spread the table
With our best cloth. There are apples,
Bright as red clocks, upon the mantel.
The snow is a weary face at the window.
How sweetly does He sleep

"Into this bitter world, O Terrible Huntsman!"
I say, and she takes my hand—"Hush,
You will wake Him."

The taste of tears is on her mouth
When I kiss her. I take an apple
And hold it tightly in my fist;
The cold, swollen face of war leans in the window.

They are blowing out the candles, Mary . . .
The world is a thing gone mad tonight.
O hold Him tenderly, dear Mother,
For His is a kingdom in the hearts of men.

KENNETH PATCHEN

NEW PRINCE, NEW POMP

Behold a silly, tender babe
  In freezing winter night,
In homely manger trembling lies:
  Alas, a piteous sight.

The inns are full; no man will yield
  This little Pilgrim bed,
But forced he is with silly beasts
  In crib to shroud His head.

Despise not Him for lying there,
  First what he is inquire;
An orient pearl is often found
  In depth of dirty mire.

Weigh not His crib, His wooden dish.
  Nor beasts that by Him feed;
Weigh not His mother's poor attire,
  Nor Joseph's simple weed.

This stable is a Prince's court.
  This crib His chair of state;
The beasts are parcel of His pomp,
  The wooden dish His plate.

The persons in that poor attire
  His royal liveries wear;
The Prince Himself is come from Heaven,
  This pomp is prizèd there.

With joy approach, O Christian wight!
  Do homage to thy King,
And highly praise His humble pomp
  Which He from Heaven doth bring.

ROBERT SOUTHWELL

A CHRISTMAS FOLK-SONG

The little Jesus came in town;
The wind blew up, the wind blew down;
Out in the street the wind was bold;
Now who would house Him from the cold?

Then opened wide a stable door,
Fair were the rushes on the floor;
The Ox put forth a hornéd head;
"Come, Little Lord, here make Thy bed."

Up rose the Sheep were folded near:
"Thou Lamb of God, come, enter here."
He entered there to rush and read,
Who was the Lamb of God indeed.

The little Jesus came to town;
With Ox and Sheep He laid Him down;
Peace to the byre, peace to the fold,
For that they housed Him from the cold!

LISETTE WOODWORTH REESE

CHRISTMAS IN THE WOOD

Tonight when the hoar frost falls on the wood,
And the rabbit cowers, and the squirrel is cold,
And the horned owl huddles against a star,
And the drifts are deep, and the year is old,
All shy creatures will think of Him.
The shivering mouse, the hare, the wild young fox,
The doe with the startled fawn,
Will dream of gentleness and a Child:

The buck with budding horns will turn
His starry eyes to a silver hill tonight,
The chipmunk will awake and stir
And leave his burrow for the chill, dark midnight,
And all timid things will pause and sigh, and sighing, bless
That Child who loves the trembling hearts,
The shy hearts of the wilderness.

FRANCES FROST

THE INN THAT MISSED ITS CHANCE
(*The landlord speaks*, A.D. 28)

What could be done? The house was full of folks!
His honor, Marcus Lucius, and his scribes
Who made the census; honorable men
From farthest Galilee, come hitherward
To be enrolled; high ladies and their lords;
The rich, the rabbis, such a noble throng
As Bethlehem had never seen before
And may not see again. And there they were,
Close-herded with their servants, till the inn
Was like a hive at swarming time, and I
Was fairly crazed among them.

                              Could I know
That they were so important? Just the two,
No servants, just a workman sort of man,
Leading a donkey, and his wife thereon
Drooping and pale,—I saw them not myself,
My servants must have driven them away;
But had I seen them,—how was I to know?
Were inns to welcome stragglers up and down
In all our towns from Beersheba to Dan,
Till He should come? And how were men to know?

There was a sign, they say, a heavenly light
Resplendent: but I had no time for stars,
And there were songs of angels in the air
Out on the hills; but how was I to hear
Amid the thousand clamors of an inn?

Of course if I had known them, who they were,
And who was He that should be born that night
For now I learn that they will make him King,
A second David, who will ransom us
From these Philistine Romans—who but He
That feeds an army with a loaf of bread,
And if a soldier falls, He but touches him
And up he leaps, uninjured? Had I known,
I would have turned the whole inn upside down,
His honor, Marcus Lucius, and the rest,
And sent them all to the stables, had I known.

So you have seen Him, stranger, and perhaps
Again may see Him? Prithee say for me,
I did not know; and if He comes again
As he will surely come, with retinue,
And banners, and an army, tell my Lord
That all my inn is His to make amends.

Alas! Alas! to miss a chance like that!
This inn might be the chief among them all.
The birthplace of the Messiah, had I known!

                                        AMOS RUSSEL WELLS

THE GUEST

Yet if His Majesty, our sovereign lord,
  Should of his own accord
  Friendly himself invite,
And say, "I'll be your guest to-morrow night,"
How should we stir ourselves, call and command
All hands to work! "Let no man idle stand!

Set me fine Spanish tables in the hall,
  See they be fitted all;
  Let there be room to eat;
And order taken that there want no meat.
See every sconce and candlestick made bright,
That without tapers they may give a light.

"Look to the presence: are the carpets spread,
  The dazie o'er the head,
  The cushions in the chairs,
And all the candles lighted on the stairs?
Perfume the chambers, and in any case
Let each man give attendance in his place!"

Thus if a king were coming would we do,
  And, 'twere good reason too;
  For 'tis a duteous thing
To show all honour to an earthly king,
And after all our travail and our cost,
So he be pleased, to think no labour lost.

But at the coming of the King of Heaven
  All's set at six and seven:
  We wallow in our sin,
Christ cannot find a chamber in the inn,
We entertain Him always like a stranger,
And, as at first, still lodge Him in a manger.

ANONYMOUS

CHRISTMAS IN FREELANDS

The Red-Bud, the Kentucky Tree,
Bloomed the spring to life for me
In Freelands; and the Mocking Bird
—Nimble chorister of glee,
Sweet as poet ever heard
In a world of ecstasy—
Sang the summer, and the sun;
Sang the summer in to me.

The spring is gone! The summer gone!
The Cardinal has gone away!
The fire-flies, dancing on the lawn,
—Each a little moon at play—
Are gone, with summer, gone away!
And, where green acres were aglow,
Daisy munches in the snow!

A snowy field! A stable piled
With straw! A donkey's sleepy pow!
A mother beaming on a child!
A manger, and a munching cow!
—These we all remember now—
And airy voices, heard afar!
And three Magicians, and a Star!

Two thousand times of snow declare
That on the Christmas of the year
There is a singing in the air;
And all who listen for it hear
A fairy chime, a seraph strain,
Telling He is born again,
—That all we love is born again.

JAMES STEPHENS

A HYMN ON THE NATIVITY OF MY SAVIOUR

I sing the birth was born tonight,
The Author both of life and light,
  The angels so did sound it;
And like the ravished shepherds said,
Who saw the light, and were afraid,
  Yet searched, and true they found it.

The Son of God, the eternal King,
That did us all salvation bring,
  And freed the soul from danger;
He whom the whole world could not take,
The Word which heaven and earth did make,
  Was now laid in a manger.

The Father's wisdom willed it so,
The Son's obedience knew no No,
Both wills were in one stature;
And as that wisdom had decreed,
The Word was now made Flesh indeed,
  And took on him our nature.

What comfort by Him do we win,
Who made Himself the price of sin,
  To make us heirs of glory!
To see this Babe, all innocence,
A Martyr born in our defense,
  Can man forget this story?

BEN JONSON

STARS IN APPLE CORES
Matthew 1:9, 10
II Corinthians 4:6
II Peter 1:19

You
are the One who put
stars
in apple cores

God
of all stars and symbols
and all grace,
You have reshaped
the empty space

deep in my apple heart
into a core of light
a star to shine
like Bethlehem's far-
to-near Night Sign:
bright
birth announcement
of Your
Day Star

LUCI SHAW

THE GROUNDHOG

The groundhog is, at best, a simple soul
   without pretension, happy in his hole,
twinkle-eyed, shy, earthy, coarse-coated grey,
   no use at all (except on Groundhog Day).
At Christmas time, a rather doubtful fable
   gives the beast standing room inside the stable
with other simple things, shepherds, and sheep,
   cows, and small winter birds, and on the heap
of warm, sun-sweetened hay, the simplest thing
   of all—a Baby. Can a groundhog sing,
or only grunt his wonder? Could he know
   this new-born Child had planned him, long ago,
for groundhog-hood? Whether true tale or fable,
   I like to think that he *was* in the stable,
part of the Plan, and that He who designed
   all simple wonderers, may have had me in mind.

LUCI SHAW

THE NATIVITY

Among the oxen (like an ox I'm slow)
I see a glory in the stable grow
Which, with the ox's dullness might at length
    Give me an ox's strength.

Among the asses (stubborn I as they)
I see my Saviour where I looked for hay;
So may my beastlike folly learn at least
    The patience of a beast.

Among the sheep (I like a sheep have strayed)
I watch the manger where my Lord is laid;
Oh that my baa-ing nature would win thence
    Some woolly innocence!

C. S. LEWIS

MORNING GLORY

In this meadow starred with spring
Shepherds kneel before their king.
Mary throned, with dreaming eyes,
Gowned in blue like rain-washed skies.

Lifts her tiny son that he
May behold their courtesy.
And green-smocked children, awed and good,
Bring him blossoms from the wood.

Clear the sunlit steeples chime
Mary's coronation-time,
Loud the happy children quire
To the golden-windowed morn;
While the lord of their desire
Sleeps below the crimson thorn.

SIEGFRIED SASSOON

THE SHEPHERD SPEAKS

Out of the midnight sky a great dawn broke,
And a voice singing flooded us with song,
In David's city was He born, it sang,
A Saviour, Christ the Lord. Then while I sat
Shivering with the thrill of that great cry,
A mighty choir a thousandfold more sweet
Suddenly sang, Glory to God, and Peace—
Peace on the earth; my heart, almost unnerved
By that swift loveliness, would hardly beat.
Speechless we waited till the accustomed night
Gave us no promise more of sweet surprise;
Then scrambling to our feet, without a word
We started through the fields to find the Child.

JOHN ERSKINE

THE SHEPHERD LEFT BEHIND

"The hour is late," the shepherds said,
"And the miles are long to wind;
Do you stay here with the sheep, instead!"
And they left the lad behind.

He heard their feet in the dark ravine,
The drop of the sheepfold bars,
And then blue stillness flowed between
The huddled sheep and stars.

He sat him down to wait for dawn,
His crook across his knees,
And thought of the shepherds moving on
Under the olive trees.

Herding his flocks in Palestine,
He thought, that lad of old,
How some must follow the Angel's sign
And some must tend the fold.

And as he mused he took his pipe—
'Twas a shepherd's pipe he had—
And there, while the frosty stars grew ripe
And shone on the shepherd lad,

The first sweet Christmas carol twined
From the willow's slender stem—
Blown by the shepherd left behind—
To a Babe in Bethlehem.

MILDRED PLEW MERRYMAN

KINGS AND STARS

As they came from the East
Following a star,

One said:
The sun burns,
The moon changes,
Stars are faithful.

One said:
They shine in all tongues,
Every heart knows them,
By starlight there are no borders.

One said:
The world widens
By starlight,
The mind reaches;
Stars beget journeys.

JOHN ERSKINE

THE MAGI

Now as at all times I can see in the mind's eye,
In their stiff, painted clothes, the pale unsatisfied ones
Appear and disappear in the blue depth of the sky
With all their ancient faces like rain-beaten stones,
And all their helms of silver hovering side by side,
And all their eyes still fixed, hoping to find once more,
Being by Calvary's turbulence unsatisfied,
The uncontrollable mystery on the bestial floor.

WILLIAM BUTLER YEATS

TO HIS SAVIOUR, A CHILD;
A PRESENT, BY A CHILD

Go pretty child and bear this Flower
Unto thy little Saviour;
And tell Him, by that Bud now blown,
He is the *Rose of Sharon* known:
When thou hast said so, stick it there
Upon his Bib, or Stomacher:
And tell him, (for good handsell too)
That thou has brought a Whistle new,
Made of a clean strait oaten reed,
To charm his cries, (at time of need:)
Tell Him, for Coral, thou hast none;
But if thou hadst, He should have one;
But poor thou art, and known to be
Even as moneyless, as He.
Lastly, if thou canst win a kiss
From those mellifluous lips of his;
Then never take a second one,
To spoil the first impression.

ROBERT HERRICK

TO A CHRISTMAS TWO-YEAR-OLD

Child, and all children,
come and celebrate
the little one who came,
threatened by hate
and Herod's sword.
Sing softly and rejoice
in the reward
for all the baby boys
of Bethlehem
who died
in Jesus' place.

Small wonder when He grew
He wanted children by His side,
stretched out His arms, stood,
beckoned you,
called *Come to me*
and died
in your place
so that you could.

LUCI SHAW

INCARNATION POEM

He did not come
a gnostic
      wholly other
masquerading as a man
dragging a phony body
through corruption.

Mary labored
      at his coming
screamed
and when the heavy stable air
shocked
     his lungs
he pierced the night
with cries.

He grew
     bulged his biceps
with childish pride
then felt his body
change
     roughen
turn angular
and hard. He felt
the pangs of adolescence
and learned to name himself
a man.

But the dove descended.
The voice pronounced
the unimaginable:
God and flesh were one.

JOHN LEAX

A MEDIEVAL POEM OF THE NATIVITY

Let us gather hand in hand
And sing of bliss without an end:
The devil has fled from earthly land,
And Son of God is made our Friend.

A Child is born in man's abode,
And in that Child no blemish showed.
That Child is God, that Child is Man,
And in that Child our life began.

Be blithe and merry, sinful man,
For your marriage peace began
   When Christ was born.
Come to Christ, your peace is due
Because He shed His blood for you,
   Who were forlorn.

Sinful man, be blithe and bold,
For heaven is both bought and sold,
   Through and through.
Come to Christ and peace foretold:
His life He gave a hundredfold
   To succor you.

So let us gather hand in hand
And sing of bliss without an end:
The devil has fled from earthly land,
And Son of God is made our Friend.

ANONYMOUS

CHRISTMAS

All after pleasures as I rid one day,
   My horse and I, both tired, body and mind,
   With full cry of affections, quite astray,
I took up in the next inn I could find.
There when I came, whom found I but my dear,
   My dearest Lord, expecting till the grief
   Of pleasures brought me to him, ready there
To be all passengers' most sweet relief?
O Thou, whose glorious, yet contracted light,
   Wrapt in night's mantle, stole into a manger;
   Since my dark soul and brutish is thy right,
To man of all beasts be not thou a stranger:
   Furnish and deck my soul, that thou mayst have
   A better lodging, than a rack or grave.

The shepherds sing; and shall I silent be?
   My God, no hymn for thee?
My soul's a shepherd too; a flock it feeds
   Of thoughts, and words, and deeds.
The pasture is thy word: the streams, thy grace
   Enriching all the place.
Shepherd and flock shall sing, and all my powers
   Outsing the daylight hours.
Then we will chide the sun for letting night
   Take up his place and right:
We sing one common Lord; wherefore he should
   Himself the candle hold.
I will go searching, till I find a sun
   Shall stay, till we have done;
A willing shiner, that shall shine as gladly,
   As frost-nipt suns look sadly.
Then we will sing, and shine all our own day,
   And one another pay:
His beams shall cheer my breast, and both so twine,
Till ev'n his beams sing, and my music shine.

GEORGE HERBERT

ECCE PUER

Of the dark past
A child is born
With joy and grief
My heart is torn

Calm in his cradle
The living lies.
May love and mercy
Unclose his eyes!

Young life is breathed
On the glass;
The world that was not
Comes to pass.

A child is sleeping:
An old man gone.
O father forsaken,
Forgive your son!

JAMES JOYCE

ADVENT

Earth grown old, yet still so green,
  Deep beneath her crust of cold
Nurses fire unfelt, unseen:
  Earth grown old.

We who live are quickly told:
Millions more lie hid between
  Inner swathings of her fold.

When will fire break up her screen?
  When will life burst thro' her mould?
Earth, earth, earth, thy cold is keen,
  Earth grown old.

CHRISTINA ROSSETTI

KARMA

Christmas was in the air and all was well
With him, but for a few confusing flaws
In divers of God's images. Because
A friend of his would neither buy nor sell,
Was he to answer for the axe that fell?
He pondered; and the reason for it was,
Partly, a slowly freezing Santa Claus
Upon the corner, with his beard and bell.

Acknowledging an improvident surprise,
He magnified a fancy that he wished
The friend whom he had wrecked were here again.
Not sure of that, he found a compromise;
And from the fulness of his heart he fished
A dime for Jesus who had died for men.

EDWARD ARLINGTON ROBINSON

THE BURNING BABE

As I in hoary winter's night stood shivering in the snow,
Surprised I was with sudden heat which made my heart to glow;
And lifting up a fearful eye to view what fire was near,
A pretty babe all burning bright did in the air appear;
Who, scorchéd with excessive heat, such floods of tears did shed,
As though his floods should quench his flames which with his tears were fed.
"Alas," quoth he, "but newly born in fiery heats I fry,
Yet none approach to warm their hearts or feel my fire but I!
My faultless breast the furnace is, the fuel wounding thorns;
Love is the fire, and sighs the smoke, the ashes shames and scorns;
The fuel justice layeth on, and mercy blows the coals;
The metal in this furnace wrought are men's defiléd souls,
For which, as now on fire I am to work them to their good,
So will I melt into a bath to wash them in my blood."
With this he vanished out of sight and swiftly shrunk away,
And straight I calléd unto mind that it was Christmas day.

ROBERT SOUTHWELL

TO JESUS ON HIS BIRTHDAY

For this your mother sweated in the cold,
For this you bled upon the bitter tree:
A yard of tinsel ribbon bought and sold;
A paper wreath; a day at home for me.
The merry bells ring out, the people kneel;
Up goes the man of God before the crowd;
With voice of honey and with eyes of steel
He drones your humble gospel to the proud.
Nobody listens. Less than the wind that blows
Are all your words to us you died to save.
O Prince of Peace! O Sharon's dewy Rose!
How mute you lie within your vaulted grave.
The stone the angel rolled away with tears
Is back upon your mouth these thousand years.

EDNA ST. VINCENT MILLAY

A CHRISTMAS HYMN

And some of the Pharisees from among the multitude said unto him,
Master, rebuke thy disciples.
And he answered and said unto them, I tell you that, if these should
hold their peace, the stones would immediately cry out.

St. Luke XIX, 39–40

A stable-lamp is lighted
Whose glow shall wake the sky;
The stars shall bend their voices,
And every stone shall cry.
And every stone shall cry,
And straw like gold shall shine;
A barn shall harbor heaven,
A stall become a shrine.

This child through David's city
Shall ride in triumph by;
The palm shall strew its branches,
And every stone shall cry.
And every stone shall cry,
Though heavy, dull, and dumb,
And lie within the roadway
To pave his kingdom come.

Yet he shall be forsaken
And yielded up to die;
The sky shall groan and darken,
And every stone shall cry.
And every stone shall cry
For stony hearts of men:
God's blood upon the spearhead,
God's love refused again.

But now, as at the ending,
The low is shifted high:
The stars shall bend their voices,
And every stone shall cry.
And every stone shall cry
In praises of the child
By whose descent among us
The worlds are reconciled.

RICHARD WILBUR

TO SEE THE CROSS AT CHRISTMAS

I

Who sees the cross at Christmas?
For there is more to see:

The decorated houses/mausolea of modern men.

The measure of prosperity and pride,
Rigid deer and stuck sleighs ride the roofs,
Gutters glare with fiery beads from edge to edge.
All is safe, until the lights go out.
Cut out cardboard figures set in place by cardboard men,
Empty plastic Santa Clauses installed by empty men.
Buy bulbs and burn!
Electric companies rejoice,
Their meters measure faith's impersonal price.
The glare interpreted to children, "So that Santa knows the way."

(God knows the way;
 He came through the glitter once before with tears.)

II

The mixed myths—matrix of modern men.

The little child was laid in straw,
Along with plastic tommy guns.
The wise men moved in from the East,
To seduce with perfume Eve on Christmas.
Dumb animals shared the savior's stall,
While visions of sugar plums danced in their heads.
Shepherds watched their flocks by night,
By day they sold electric trains and ate cold sandwiches.
Herod's anger stemmed from fear,
That Saint Nicholas soon would be here.

God is confused; With Santa Claus
The mind God gave you went to sleep,
Depression's way to save the day
Ignoring night;
Shaving facts and mixing myths into a pleasing harmony.
A potpourri apart from pain,
Enough for you—Who cannot see the cross at Christmas

III

Substituting gifts—the measure of modern men.

The registers ring out glad tidings of great joy
    For skillful hucksters wading through piles of paper tape.

The customer is quite content
To know which way his savings went
—but not his self.

His guilt for having hurt is healed,
Transformed to toys and clothes,
And signs of deep affection
—with a price tag.

His generosity becomes a reputation,
Giving gifts a personhood,
Ways to avoid the final confrontation
—the giving of himself.

Conscience' price is paid,
Guilt allayed
—gifts are given.
His self protected,
The world is safe again for him—

Who cannot see the cross at Christmas.

IV

Our sense for what is real is nearly dead.
The palliative powers, summoned at this season
Are in themselves a light,
And a way of life.

God hears your soft and unconditioned prayer:
"Don't hurt me more,
Or spoil my joy,
Or take away my feeling for a while.
Life is so drab.
I've been so hurt,
That it feels good for a while to live a lie.
It's better than my weekly work,
Or facing what I am."

For in our hearts we know that God is dead,
And that is why we decorate our houses
    —to fill the void;
That is why we mix our myths
    —to color up his corpse;
That is why we now give gifts of things
    —and retain our selves.

God is dead.
He does not require anything of us,
    —anymore.

Behind the fabric of distortion
Is the coherence of the truth:
That all our ways are pendulous runs,
And in the end are bound to fail
Because they don't exist.

And God's enfleshment is the key:

The way he chose to be with us
Made him too thick to be seen.
God cannot be real and opaque.
God cannot be born and die.
God cannot love and work his will with weakness.
God cannot.
We will not let him, You and I.

A crib,
A cross,
An empty tomb,
The signs of God's decisive difference for the world,
That makes you free to cross the room,
And cross the world—

    To see the cross at Christmas.

ROGER COOPER

MUSÉE DES BEAUX ARTS

About suffering they were never wrong,
The Old Masters: how well they understood
Its human position; how it takes place
While someone else is eating or opening a window or just walking
    dully along;
How, when the aged are reverently, passionately waiting
For the miraculous birth, there always must be
Children who did not specially want it to happen, skating
On a pond at the edge of the wood:
They never forgot
That even the dreadful martyrdom must run its course
Anyhow in a corner, some untidy spot
Where the dogs go on with their doggy life and the torturer's horse
Scratches its innocent behind on a tree.

In Breughel's *Icarus*, for instance: how everything turns away
Quite leisurely from the disaster; the ploughman may
Have heard the splash, the forsaken cry,
But for him it was not an important failure; the sun shone
As it had to on the white legs disappearing into the green
Water; and the expensive delicate ship that must have seen
Something amazing, a boy falling out of the sky,
Had somewhere to get to and sailed calmly on.

W. H. AUDEN

A CHRISTMAS PRAYER

O God, our loving Father, help us
Rightly to remember the birth of Jesus,
That we may share in the song of the
Angels, the gladness of the shepherds
And the worship of the wise men.

Close the door of hate and open the
Door of love all over the world.

Deliver us from evil by the blessing
That Christ brings, and teach us
To be merry with clear hearts.

May the Christmas morning make us happy
To be thy children and the Christmas
Evening bring us to our beds with
Grateful thoughts, forgiving, and
Forgiven, for Jesus' sake. Amen.

ROBERT LOUIS STEVENSON

The Cross and the Resurrection

THE AGONY IN THE GARDEN

He knelt, the Savior knelt and prayed,
  When but His Father's eye
Looked through the lonely garden's shade
  On that dread agony;
The Lord All above, beneath,
Was bowed with sorrow unto death.

The sun set in a fearful hour,
  The stars might well grow dim,
When this mortality had power
  So to o'ershadow Him!
That He who gave man's breath, might know
The very depths of human woe.

He proved them all!—the doubt, the strife,
  The faint perplexing dread,
The mists that hang o'er parting life,
  All gathered round his head;
And the Deliverer knelt to pray—
Yet passed it not, that cup, away!

It passed not—though the stormy wave
  Had sunk beneath His tread;
It passed not—though to Him the grave
  Had yielded up its dead.
But there was sent Him from on high
A gift of strength for man to die.

And was the sinless thus beset
  With anguish and dismay?
How may we meet our conflict yet
  In the dark narrow way?
Through Him—through Him, that path who trod—
Save, or we perish, Son of God!

FELICIA HEMANS

THE LAST DEFILE

Make us Thy mountaineers;
We would not linger on the lower slope,
Fill us afresh with hope, O God of Hope,
Than undefeated we may climb the hill
As seeing Him who is invisible.

Let us die climbing. When this little while
Lies far behind us, and the last defile
Is all alight, and in that light we see
Our Leader and our Lord, what will it be?

AMY CARMICHAEL

WEDNESDAY IN HOLY WEEK

Man's life is death. Yet Christ endured to live
　Preaching and teaching, toiling to and fro,
Few men accepting what he yearned to give,
　Few men with eyes to know
　His face, that Face of Love he stooped to show.

Man's death is life. For Christ endured to die
　In slow unuttered weariness of pain,
A curse and an astonishment, passed by,
　Pointed at, mocked again
　By men for whom he shed his blood—in vain?

CHRISTINA ROSSETTI

SIMON THE CYRENIAN SPEAKS

He never spoke a word to me,
And yet He called my name,
He never gave a sign to see,
And yet I knew and came.

At first I said, "I will not bear,
His cross upon my back—
He only seeks to place it there
Because my skin is black."

But He was dying for a dream,
And He was very meek;
And in His eyes there shone a
     gleam
Men journey far to seek.

It was Himself my pity bought;
I did for Christ alone
What all of Rome could not have
     wrought
With bruise of lash or stone.

COUNTEE CULLEN

THE INCARNATION AND PASSION

Lord! when thou didst thy self undress
Laying by thy robes of glory,
To make us more, thou wouldst be less,
And becam'st a woeful story.

To put on Clouds instead of light,
And clothe the morning-star with dust,
Was a translation of such height
As, but in thee, was ne'er expressed;

Brave worms, and Earth! that thus could have
A God Enclosed within your Cell,
Your maker pent up in a grave,
Life locked in death, heaven in a shell;

Ah, my dear Lord! what couldst thou spy
In this impure, rebellious clay,
That made thee thus resolve to die
For those that kill thee every day?

O what strange wonders could thee move
To slight thy precious blood, and breath!
Sure it was *Love*, my Lord; for *Love*
Is only stronger far than death.

HENRY VAUGHAN

A QUINTINA OF CROSSES

Beyond, beneath, within, wherever blood,
If there were blood, flows with the pulse of love,
Where God's circle and all orbits cross,
Through the black space of death to baby life
Came God, planting the secret genes of God.

By the permission of a maiden's love,
Love came upon the seeds of words, broke blood,
And howled into the Palestine of life,
A baby roiled by memories of God.
Sometimes he smiled, sometimes the child was cross.

Often at night he dreamed a dream of God
And was the dream he dreamed. Often across
The lily fields he raged and lived their life,
And heaven's poison festered in his blood,
Loosing the passion of unthinkable love.

But mostly, though, he lived a prentice's life
Until a singing in the surge of blood,
Making a chorus of the genes of God,
Flailed him into the tempest of a love
That lashed the North Star and the Southern Cross.

His neighbors smelled an alien in his blood,
A secret enemy and double life;
He was a mutant or an obscene cross
Outraging decency with naked love.
He stripped the last rags from a proper God

The life of God must blood this cross for love.

CHAD WALSH

CRAFTSMAN

Carpenter's son, carpenter's son,
is the wood fine
and smoothly sanded, or rough-grained,
lying along your back? Was it well-planed?
Did they use
a plumbline
when they set you up? Is the angle true?
Why did they choose
that dark, expensive stain
to gloss the timbers
next to your feet and fingers? You
should know—who,
Joseph-trained, judged all trees
for special service.

Carpenter's son, carpenter's son,
were the nails new and cleanly driven
when the dark hammers sang?
Is the earth warped from where you hang,
high enough for a world view?

Carpenter's son, carpenter's son,
was it a job well done?

LUCI SHAW

MY GOD, MY GOD, LOOK UPON ME.
—VERSE 1

And God looked down at God that day,
And God looked up and tried to pray.

He prayed to nothing he could see.
"Father," he said, "look down at me."

It was the strangest of his days.
He could not see the Father's gaze.

He could not hear the Father speak.
He felt his own lips growing weak.

He saw the brightness drain from sky.
He saw the noon darken and die.

He saw the soldiers playing dice.
He told a thief of Paradise.

He gave a mother to a son.
He knew and said the day was done.

He drank the darkness, and he said,
"Into thy hands," and he was dead.

CHAD WALSH
From *The Psalm of Christ*

BALLAD OF THE GOODLY FERE

Simon Zelotes speaketh it somewhile
after the Crucifixion.

Ha' we lost the goodliest fere o' all
For the priests and the gallows tree?
Aye lover he was of brawny men,
O' ships and the open sea.

When they came wi' a host to take Our Man
His smile was good to see,
"First let these go!" quo' our Goodly Fere,
"Or I'll see ye damned," says he.

Aye he sent us out through the crossed high spears
And the scorn of his laugh rang free,
"Why took ye not me when I walked about
Alone in the town?" says he.

Oh we drank his "Hale" in the good red wine
When we last made company,
No capon priest was the Goodly Fere
But a man o' men was he.

I ha' seen him drive a hundred men
Wi' a bundle o' cords swung free,
When they took the high and holy house
For their pawn and treasury.

They'll no' get him a' in a book I think
Though they write it cunningly;
No mouse of the scrolls was the Goodly Fere
But aye loved the open sea.

If they think they ha' snared our Goodly Fere
They are fools to the last degree.
"I'll go to the feast," quo' our Goodly Fere,
"Though I go to the gallows tree."

"Ye ha' seen me heal the lame and blind,
And wake the dead," says he,
"Ye shall see one thing to master all:
'Tis how a brave man dies on the tree."

A son of God was the Goodly Fere
That bade us his brother be.
I ha' seen him cow a thousand men.
I have seen him upon the tree.

He cried no cry when they drave the nails
And the blood gushed hot and free,
The hounds of the crimson sky gave tongue
But never a cry cried he.

I ha' seen him cow a thousand men
On the hills o' Galilee,
They whined as he walked out calm between,
Wi' his eyes like the gray o' the sea.

Like the sea that brooks no voyaging
With the winds unleashed and free,
Like the sea that he cowed at Genseret
Wi' twey words spoke' suddently.

A master of men was the Goodly Fere,
A mate of the wind and sea,
If they think they ha' slain our Goodly Fere

They are fools eternally.
I ha' seen him eat o' the honey-comb
Sin' they nailed him to the tree.

EZRA POUND

ON OUR CRUCIFIED LORD NAKED AND BLOODY

They have left Thee naked, Lord, O that they had;
This garment too I would they had denied.
Thee with Thyself they have too richly clad,
Opening the purple wardrobe of Thy side.
   O never could be found garments too good
For Thee to wear, but these of Thine own blood.

RICHARD CRASHAW

CHRIST IS ARISEN

Christ is arisen.
  Joy to thee, mortal!
Out of His prison,
  Forth from its portal!
Christ is not sleeping,
  Seek Him no longer;
Strong was His keeping,
  Jesus was stronger.

Christ is arisen.
  Seek Him not here;
Lonely His prison,
  Empty His bier;

Vain His entombing,
  Spices and lawn,
Vain the perfuming,
  Jesus is gone.

Christ is arisen.
  Joy to thee, mortal!
Empty His prison,
  Broken its portal!
Rising, He giveth
  His shroud to the sod;
Risen, He liveth,
  And liveth to God.

J. W. VON GOETHE

HYMN FOR EASTER MORN

Light's glittering morn bedecks the sky,
Heaven thunders forth its victor-cry;
The glad earth shouts its triumph high,
And groaning hell makes wild reply.

While He, the King of glorious might,
Treads down Death's strength in Death's despite,
And trampling hell by victor's right
Brings forth His sleeping saints to light.

Fast barred beneath the stone of late,
In watch and ward where soldiers wait,
Now, shining in triumphant state,
He rises victor from death's gate.

Hell's pains are loosed and tears are fled;
Captivity is captive led:
The angel, crowned with light, hath said:
"The Lord is risen from the dead."

92

The Apostles' hearts were full of pain
For their dear Lord so lately slain,
That Lord his servants' wicked train
With bitter scorn had dared arraign.

With gentle voice the Angel gave
The women tidings at the grave:
"Forthwith your Master shall ye see:
He goes before to Galilee."

And while with fear and joy they pressed
To tell these tidings to the rest,
Their Lord, their living Lord, they meet
And see his form and kiss his feet.

The eleven, when they hear, with speed
To Galilee forthwith proceed,
That there they may behold once more
The Lord's dear face, as oft before.

In this our bright and Paschal day
The sun shines out with purer ray,
When Christ, to earthly sight made plain,
The glad Apostles see again.

The wounds, the riven wounds He shows
In that His flesh with light that glows,
With public voice both far and nigh,
The Lord's arising testify.

O Christ, the King who lov'st to bless,
Do thou our hearts and souls possess;
To Thee our praise that we may pay,
To whom our laud is due—for aye.

ANONYMOUS

THE DAY OF RESURRECTION

The day of resurrection!
  Earth, tell it out abroad;
The Passover of gladness,
  The Passover of God
From death to life eternal,
  From this world to the sky,
Our Christ hath brought us over
  With hymns of victory!

Our hearts be pure from evil,
  That we may see aright
The Lord in rays eternal
  Of resurrection light;

And, list'ning to His accents,
  May hear, so calm and plain,
His own, "All hail!" and, hearing,
  May raise the victor-strain.

Now let the heav'ns be joyful,
  Let earth her song begin,
Let the round world keep triumph,
  And all that is therein;
Let all things seen and unseen
  Their notes in gladness blend;
For Christ the Lord hath risen,
  Our Joy that hath no end. Amen.

JOHN OF DAMASCUS

EASTER

Rise heart; thy Lord is risen. Sing His praise
    Without delays,
Who takes thee by the hand, that thou likewise
    With Him mayst rise:
That as His death calcined thee to dust,
His life may make thee gold, and much more, just.

Awake, my lute, and struggle for thy part
    With all thy art.
The cross taught all wood to resound His Name,
    Who bore the same.
His stretched sinews taught all strings what key
Is best to celebrate this most high day.

Consort both heart and lute, and twist a song
    Pleasant and long:
Or, since all music is but three parts vied
    And multiplied,
O let Thy blessed Spirit bear a part,
And make up our defects with His sweet art.

        GEORGE HERBERT

THE TRAVAIL OF PASSION

When the flaming lute-thronged angelic door is wide;
When an immortal passion breathes in mortal clay;
Our hearts endure the scourge, the plaited thorns, the way
Crowded with bitter faces, the wounds in palm and side,
The vinegar-heavy sponge, the flowers by Kedron stream;
We will bend down and loosen our hair over you,
That it may drop faint perfume, and be heavy with dew,
Lilies of death-pale hope, roses of passionate dream.

       WILLIAM BUTLER YEATS

THE CHOICE OF THE CROSS

Hard it is, very hard,
To travel up the slow and stony road
To Calvary, to redeem mankind; far better
To make but one resplendent miracle,
Lean through the cloud, lift the right hand of power
And with a sudden lightning smite the world perfect.
Yet this was not God's way, Who had the power,
But set it by, choosing the cross, the thorn,
The sorrowful wounds. Something there is, perhaps,
That power destroys in passing, something supreme,
To whose great value in the eyes of God
That cross, that thorn, and those five wounds bear witness.

DOROTHY L. SAYERS
From *The Devil to Pay*

A HYMN TO GOD THE FATHER

Hear me, O God!
  A broken heart
  Is my best part:
Use still Thy rod,
  That I may prove,
  Therein, Thy love.

If Thou hadst not
  Been stern to me,
  But left me free,
I had forgot
  Myself and Thee.

For, sin's so sweet,
  As minds ill-bent
  Rarely repent,
Until they meet
  Their punishment.

Who more can crave
  Than Thou hast done?
  That gav'st a Son,
To free a slave
  First made of naught,
  With all since bought.

Sin, death, and hell
  His glorious Name
  Quite overcame;
Yet I rebel,
  And slight the same.

But, I'll come in
  Before my loss
  Me farther toss,
As sure to win
  Under His cross.

BEN JONSON

EASTER WINGS

Lord, who createdst man in wealth and store,
  Though foolishly he lost the same,
    Decaying more and more
      Till he became
      Most poor:
      With Thee
      O let me rise
    As larks, harmoniously,
  And sing this day Thy victories:
Then shall the fall further the flight in me.

My tender age in sorrow did begin:
  And still with sickness and shame
    Thou didst so punish sin
      That I became
      Most thin.
      With Thee
    Let me combine,
  And feel this day Thy victory;
For, if I imp my wing on Thine,
Affliction shall advance the flight in me.

GEORGE HERBERT

ASH WEDNESDAY

My God, my God, have mercy on my sin,
For it is great; and if I should begin
To tell it all, the day would be too small
    To tell it in.

My God, Thou wilt have mercy on my sin
For Thy Love's sake: yea, if I should begin
To tell Thee all, the day would be too small
    To tell it in.

CHRISTINA ROSSETTI

REDEMPTION

Having been tenant long to a rich Lord,
   Not thriving, I resolved to be bold,
   And make a suit unto him, to afford
A new small-rented lease, and cancel th' old.
In heaven at his manour I him sought:
   They told me there, that he was lately gone
   About some land, which he had dearly bought
Long since on earth, to take possession.
I straight return'd, and knowing his great birth,
   Sought him accordingly in great resorts;
   In cities, theatres, gardens, parks, and courts:
At length I heard a ragged noise and mirth
   Of thieves and murderers: there I him espied,
   Who straight, "Your suit is granted," said, and died.

GEORGE HERBERT

SEVEN STANZAS AT EASTER

Make no mistake: if He rose at all
it was as His body;
if the cells' dissolution did not reverse, the molecules
    reknit, the amino acids rekindle,
the Church will fall.

It was not as the flowers,
each soft Spring recurrent;
it was not as His Spirit in the mouths and fuddled
    eyes of the eleven apostles;
it was as His flesh: ours.

The same hinged thumbs and toes,
the same valved heart
that—pierced—died, withered, paused, and then
    regathered out of enduring Might
new strength to enclose.

98

Let us not mock God with metaphor,
analogy, sidestepping, transcendence;
making of the event a parable, a sign painted in the
        faded credulity of earlier ages:
let us walk through the door.

The stone is rolled back, not papier-mache,
not a stone in a story,
but the vast rock of materiality that in the slow
        grinding of time will eclipse for each of us
the wide light of day.

And if we will have an angel at the tomb,
make it a real angel,
weighty with Max Planck's quanta, vivid with hair,
        opaque in the dawn light, robed in real linen
spun on a definite loom.

Let us not seek to make it less monstrous,
for our own convenience, our own sense of beauty,
lest, awakened in one unthinkable hour, we are
        embarrassed by the miracle,
and crushed by remonstrance.

                                        JOHN UPDIKE

WHY HAST THOU FORSAKEN ME?
—VERSE 1

Perhaps the Socrates he had never read,
The Socrates that Socrates poorly understood,
Had the answer. From opposites, opposites
Are generated. Cold to heat, heat to cold,
Life to death, and death to life. Perhaps the grave's
Obscenity is the womb, the only one
For the glorified body. It may be
Darkness alone, darkness, black and mute,
Void of God and a human smile, filled
With hateful laughter, dirty jokes, rattling dice,
Can empty the living room of all color
So that the chromatic slide of salvation
Fully possesses the bright screen of vision.

Or perhaps, being Man, it was simply
He must first go wherever man had been,
To whatever caves of loneliness, whatever
Caverns of no light, deep damp darkness,
Dripping walls of the spirit, man has known.

I have called to God and heard no answer,
I have seen the thick curtain drop, and sunlight die;
My voice has echoed back, a foolish voice,
The prayer restored intact to its silly source.
I have walked in darkness, he hung in it.
In all of my mines of night, he was there first;
In whatever dead tunnel I am lost, he finds me.
My God, my God, why hast thou forsaken me?
From his perfect darkness a voice says, I have not.

CHAD WALSH
From *The Psalm of Christ*

... FOR THEY SHALL SEE GOD.
MATT. 5:8

*"They only saw Jesus—and then but the outside Jesus, or a
little more. They were not pure in heart. . . . They saw Him
with their eyes, but not with those eyes which alone can see
God . . . the thought-eyes, the truth-eyes, the love-eyes can see
Him."* —George Macdonald

Christ risen was rarely recognized by sight.
They had to get beyond the way he looked.
Evidence stronger than his voice and face and footstep
waited to grow in them, to guide their groping
out of despair, their stretching toward belief.

We are as blind as they
until the opening of our deeper eyes
shows us the hands that bless and break
our bread, until we finger
wounds that tell our healing, or witness
a miracle of fish, dawn-caught
after our long night of empty nets. Handling
his word we feel his flesh, his bones, and hear
his voice saying our early-morning name.

LUCI SHAW

MY SOUL THIRSTS FOR GOD

I thirst, but not as once I did,
The vain delights of earth to share;
Thy wounds, Emmanuel, all forbid
That I should seek my pleasures there.

It was the sight of Thy dear cross
First weaned my soul from earthly things;
And taught me to esteem as dross
The mirth of fools, and pomp of kings.

I want that grace that springs from Thee,
That quickens all things where it flows;
And makes a wretched thorn, like me,
Bloom as the myrtle, or the rose.

Dear fountain of delights unknown!
No longer sink below the brim;
But overflow and pour me down
A living and life-giving stream!

For sure, of all the plants that share
The notice of Thy Father's eye;
None proves less grateful to His care
Or yields him meaner fruit than I.

WILLIAM COWPER

LONG BARREN

Thou who didst hang upon a barren tree,
My God, for me;
   Though I till now be barren, now at length,
   Lord, give me strength
To bring forth fruit to Thee.

Thou who didst bear for me the crown of thorn,
Spitting and scorn;
   Though I till now have put forth thorns,
      yet now
   Strengthen me Thou
That better fruit be borne.

Thou Rose of Sharon, Cedar of broad roots,
Vine of sweet fruits,
   Thou Lily of the vale with fadeless leaf,
   Of thousands Chief,
Feed Thou my feeble shoots.

CHRISTINA ROSSETTI

THAT DAY

That day the
words
formed
not in my mind
but on my lips

a bird hung
silently

in the sky
and the Word
burned
my tongue
like a flaming
Host

until
my eyes boiled

JOHN LEAX

AT COMMUNION

Whether I kneel or stand or sit in prayer
I am not caught in time nor held in space,
But, thrust beyond this posture, I am where
Time and eternity are face to face;
Infinity and space meet in this place
Where crossbar and upright hold the One
In agony and in all Love's embrace.
The power in helplessness which was begun
When all the brilliance of the flaming sun
Contained itself in the small confines of a child
Now comes to me in this strange action done
In mystery. Break time, break space, O wild
And lovely power. Break me: thus am I dead,
Am resurrected now in wine and bread.

MADELEINE L'ENGLE

Christ Triumphant

THE PILLAR OF THE CLOUD

Lead, kindly light, amid the encircling gloom,
    Lead thou me on!
The night is dark and I am far from home;
    Lead thou me on!
Keep thou my feet; I do not ask to see
The distant scene; one step enough for me.

I was not ever thus, nor prayed that thou
    Shouldst lead me on;
I loved to choose the path and see my path; but now
    Lead thou me on!
I loved the garish day, and, spite of fears,
Pride ruled my will; remember not past years.

So long thy power has blessed me, sure it still
    Will lead me on,
O'er moor and fen, o'er crag and torrent till
    The night is gone;
And with the morn those angel faces smile
Which I have loved long since, and lost awhile!

JOHN HENRY NEWMAN

THIS DAY BE WITH ME

This day be with me, Lord, when I go forth,
Be nearer to me than I am able to ask.
In merriment, in converse, or in task,
Walking the street, listening to men of worth,
Or greeting such as only talk and bask,
Be thy thought still my waiting soul around,
And if he come, I shall be watching found.

GEORGE MACDONALD
From *Diary of an Old Soul*

106

CANA

"This beginning of miracles did
Jesus in Cana of Galilee."

Once when our eyes were clean as noon, our rooms
Filled with the joys of Cana's feast:
For Jesus came, and His disciples, and His Mother,
And after them the singers
And some men with violins.

Once when our minds were Galilees,
And clean as skies our faces,
Our simple rooms were charmed with sun.

Our thoughts went in and out in whiter coats than
    God's disciples',
In Cana's crowded rooms, at Cana's tables.

Nor did we seem to fear the wine would fail:
For ready, in a row, to fill with water and a miracle,
We saw our earthen vessels, waiting empty.
What wine those humble waterjars foretell!

Wine for the ones who, bended to the dirty earth,
Have feared, since lovely Eden, the sun's fire,
Yet hardly mumble, in their dusty mouths, one
    prayer.

Wine for old Adam, digging in the briars!

THOMAS MERTON

THE GREAT WAGER

How is it proved?
It isn't proved, you fool! it can't be proved.
How can you prove a victory before
It's won? How can you prove a man who leads
To be a leader worth the following,
Unless you follow to the death, and out
Beyond mere death, which is not anything
But Satan's lie upon eternal life?
Well—God's my leader, and I hold that He
Is good, and strong enough to work His plan
And purpose out to its appointed end.

I walk in crowded streets, where men
And women, mad with lust, loose-lipped, and lewd,
Go promenading down to Hell's wide gates;
Yet have I looked into my mother's eyes
And seen the light that never was on sea
Or land, the light of love, pure love and true,
And on that love I bet my life. . . .

. . . I bet life on beauty, truth,
And love! not abstract, but incarnate truth;
Not beauty's passing shadow, but its self,
Its very self made flesh—love realized.
I bet my life on Christ, Christ crucified,
Aye risen, and alive forevermore.

G. A. STUDDERT-KENNEDY

HYMN FOR THE CLOSE OF THE WEEK

O what their joy and their glory must be,
Those endless sabbaths the blessed ones see;
Crown for the valiant, to weary ones rest;
God shall be all and in all ever blest.

What are the Monarch, His court and His throne?
What are the peace and the joy that they own?
Tell us, ye blessed, that in it have share;
If what ye feel ye can fully declare.

Truly Jerusalem name we that shore,
Vision of peace, that brings joy evermore;
Wish and fulfilment can severed be ne'er,
Nor the thing prayed for come short of the prayer.

We, whom no trouble distraction can bring,
Safely the anthems of Sion shall sing;
While for Thy grace, Lord, their voices of praise
Thy blessed people shall evermore raise.

There dawns no sabbath; no sabbath is o'er;
Those sabbath-keepers have one and no more;
One and unending is that triumph-song
Which to the angels and us shall belong.

Now, in the meanwhile, with hearts raised on high
We for that country must yearn and must sigh;
Seeking Jerusalem, dear native land,
Through our long exile on Babylon's strand.

Low before Him with our praises we fall,
Of whom and in whom and through whom are all:
Of whom, the Father; and in whom the Son;
Through whom, the Spirit, with these ever one.

ABELARD

109

ASCENSION HYMN

Dust and clay
Man's ancient wear!
Here you must stay,
But I elsewhere;
Souls sojourn here, but may not
    rest;
Who will ascend, must be undrest.

And yet some
That know to die
Before death come,
Walk to the sky
Even in this life; but all such can
Leave behind them the old Man.

If a star
Should leave the
    Sphere,
She must first mar
Her flaming wear,
And after fall, for in her dress
Of glory, she cannot transgress.

Man of old
Within the line
Of *Eden* could
Like the Sun shine
All naked, innocent and bright,
And intimate with Heav'n, as light;

But since he
That brightness soiled,
His garments be
All dark and spoiled,
And here are left as nothing worth,
Till the Refiner's fire breaks forth.

Then comes he!
Whose mighty light
Made his clothes be
Like Heav'n, all bright;
The Fuller, whose pure blood did
    flow
To make stained man more white
    than snow.

He alone
And none else can
Bring bone to bone
And rebuild man,
And by his all subduing might
Make clay ascend more quick than
    light.

HENRY VAUGHAN
From *Silex Scintillans*, Part II

HEAVEN

O, who will show me those delights on high?
    Echo I.
Thou Echo, thou art mortal, all men know.
    Echo No.
Wert thou not born among the trees and leaves?
    Echo Leaves.
And are there any leaves, that still abide?
    Echo Bide.
What leaves are they? Impart the matter wholly.
    Echo Holy.
Are holy leaves the Echo then of bliss?
    Echo Yes.
Then tell me, what is that supreme delight?
    Echo Light.
Light to the mind: what shall the will enjoy?
    Echo Joy.
But are there cares and business with the pleasure?
    Echo Leisure.
Light, joy, and leisure; but shall they perséver?
    Echo Ever.

         GEORGE HERBERT

PEACE

My Soul, there is a country
 Far beyond the stars,
Where stands a wingèd sentry
 All skillful in the wars,
There above noise and danger
 Sweet Peace sits crowned with
  smiles,
And One born in a manger
 Commands the beauteous files,
He is thy gracious Friend,
 And (O my soul awake!)

Did in pure love descend
 To die here for thy sake,
If thou canst get but thither,
 There grows the flower of Peace,
The Rose that cannot wither,
 Thy fortress, and thy ease;
Leave then thy foolish ranges;
 For none can thee secure,
But One, who never changes,
 Thy God, thy life, thy cure.

         HENRY VAUGHAN

EARTH BREAKS UP

Earth breaks up, time drops away,
In flows heaven, with its new day
Of endless life, when He who trod,
Very man and very God,
This Earth in weakness, shame and pain,
Dying the death whose signs remain
Up yonder on the accursed tree—
Shall come again, no more to be
Of captivity the thrall,
But the one God, All in all,
King of kings and Lord of lords,
As his servant John received the words,
"I died, and live forevermore!"

ROBERT BROWNING
From "Christmas Eve"

The Holy Spirit and the
Body of Christ

HYMN TO THE HOLY SPIRIT

Holy Spirit, Lord of light,
From thy clear celestial height
  Thy pure beaming radiance give;
Come, thou Father of the poor,
Come, with treasures that endure,
  Come, thou light of all that live!

Thou, of all consolers best,
Thou, the soul's delightsome guest,
  Dost refreshing peace bestow;
Thou in toil art comfort sweet,
Pleasant coolness in the heat,
  Solace in the midst of woe.

STEPHEN LANGTON

LOVE (III)

Love bade me welcome: yet my soul drew back,
      Guilty of dust and sin.
But quick-eyed Love, observing me grow slack
      From my first entrance in,
Drew nearer to me, sweetly questioning,
      If I lacked anything.

"A guest," I answered, "worthy to be here":
      Love said, "You shall be he."
"I the unkind, ungrateful? Ah my dear,
      I cannot look on thee."
Love took my hand, and smiling did reply,
      "Who made the eyes but I?"

"Truth, Lord; but I have marred them; let my shame
      Go where it doth deserve."
"And know you not," says Love, "who bore the blame?"
      "My dear, then I will serve."
"You must sit down," says Love, "and taste my meat:"
      So I did sit and eat.
      Finis
      Glory be to God on high
      And on earth peace
      Good will towards men

GEORGE HERBERT

PEACE

When will you ever, Peace, wild wooddove, shy wings shut,
Your round me roaming end, and under be my boughs?
When, when Peace, will you, Peace? I'll not play hypocrite
To own my heart: I yield you do come sometimes; but
That piecemeal peace is poor peace. What pure peace allows
Alarms of wars, the daunting wars, the death of it?
O surely, reaving Peace, my Lord should leave in lieu
Some good! And so he does leave Patience exquisite,
That plumes to Peace thereafter. And when Peace here does house
He comes with work to do, he does not come to coo,
        He comes to brood and sit.

GERARD MANLEY HOPKINS

SUNDAY

        O day most calm, most bright,
    The fruit of this, the next world's bud,
    Th' indorsement of supreme delight,
    Writ by a friend, and with his blood;
    The couch of time, care's balm and bay,
    The week were dark, but for thy light:
        Thy torch doth show the way.

        The other days and thou
    Make up one man, whose face thou art,
    Knocking at heaven with thy brow.
    The worky-days are the back-part;
    The burden of the week lies there,
    Making the whole to stoop and bow,
        Till thy release appear.

Man had straight forward gone
To endless death; but thou dost pull
And turn us round to look on one
Whom, if we were not very dull,
We could not choose but look on still;
Since there is no place so alone
  The which he doth not fill.

Sundays the pillars are,
On which heav'n's palace arched lies:
The other days fill up the spare
And hollow room with vanities.
They are the fruitful beds and borders
In God's rich garden: that is bare,
  Which parts their ranks and orders.

The Sundays of man's life,
Threaded together on time's string,
Make bracelets to adorn the wife
Of the eternal glorious King.
On Sunday heaven's gate stands ope',
Blessings are plentiful and rife,
  More plentiful than hope.

This day my Saviour rose,
And did inclose this light for his:
That, as each beast his manger knows,
Man might not of his fodder miss.
Christ hath took in this piece of ground,
And made a garden there for those
  Who want herbs for their wound.

The rest of our Creation
Our great Redeemer did remove
With the same shake, which at his passion
Did th' earth and all things with it move.
As Samson bore the doors away,
Christ's hands though nailed, wrought our salvation,
  And did unhinge that day.

The brightness of that day
We sullied by our foul offence;
Wherefore that robe we cast away,
Having a new at his expense,
Whose drops of blood paid the full price,
That was required to make us gay,
    And fit for Paradise.

Thou art a day of mirth;
And where the weekdays trail on ground,
Thy flight is higher, as thy birth.
O let me take thee at the bound,
Leaping with thee from sev'n to sev'n,
Till that we both, being tossed from earth,
    Fly hand in hand to heav'n.

GEORGE HERBERT

DECAY OF PIETY

Oft have I seen, ere Time had ploughed my cheek,
Matrons and Sires—who, punctual to the call
Of their loved Church, on fast or festival
Through the long year the house of Prayer would seek:
By Christmas snows, by visitation bleak
Of Easter winds; unscared, from hut or hall
They came to lowly bench or sculptured stall,
But with one fervour of devotion meek.
I see the places where they once were known,
And ask, surrounded even by kneeling crowds,
Is ancient Piety for ever flown?
Alas! even then they seemed like fleecy clouds
That, struggling through the western sky, have won
Their pensive light from a departed sun!

WILLIAM WORDSWORTH

THE SOUL OF JESUS IS RESTLESS

The soul of Jesus is restless today;
Christ is tramping through the spirit-world,
Compassion in His heart for the fainting millions;
He trudges through China, through Poland,
Through Russia, Austria, Germany, Armenia;
Patiently He pleads with the Church,
Tenderly He woos her.
The wounds of His body are bleeding afresh for the sorrows
      of His shepherdless people.
We besiege Him with selfish petitions,
We weary Him with our petty ambitions,
From the needy we bury Him in piles of carven stone,
We obscure Him in the smoke of stuffy incense,
We drown His voice with the snarls and shrieks of our disgruntled
      bickerings,
We build temples to Him with hands that are bloody,
We deny Him in the needs and sorrows of the exploited—
      "least of His brethren."
The soul of Jesus is restless today,
But eternally undismayed.

CYPRUS R. MITCHELL

FIRST-DAY THOUGHTS

In calm and cool and silence, once again
   I find my old accustomed place among
   My brethren, where, perchance, no human tongue
   Shall utter words; where never hymn is sung,
   Nor deep-toned organ blown, nor censer swung,
Nor dim light falling through the pictured pane!
There, syllabled by silence, let me hear
The still small voice which reached the prophet's ear;
Read in my heart a still diviner law
Than Israel's leader on his tables saw!
There let me strive with each besetting sin
   Recall my wandering fancies, and restrain
   The sore disquiet of a restless brain;
   And, as the path of duty is made plain,
May grace be given that I may walk therein,
   Not like the hireling, for his selfish gain,
With backward glances and reluctant tread,
Making a merit of his coward dread,
   But, cheerful, in the light around me thrown,
   Walking as one to pleasant service led;
   Doing God's will as if it were my own,
Yet trusting not in mine, but in his strength alone!

JOHN GREENLEAF WHITTIER

THE DESTRUCTION OF SENNACHERIB

I

The Assyrian came down like the wolf on the fold,
And his cohorts were gleaming in purple and gold;
And the sheen of their spears was like stars on the sea,
When the blue wave rolls nightly on deep Galilee.

II

Like the leaves of the forest when Summer is green,
That host with their banners at sunset were seen:
Like the leaves of the forest when Autumn hath blown,
That host on the morrow lay wither'd and strown.

III

For the Angel of Death spread his wings on the blast,
And breathed in the face of the foe as he passed;
And the eyes of the sleepers waxed deadly and chill,
And their hearts but once heaved, and for ever grew still!

IV

And there lay the steed with his nostril all wide,
But through it there rolled not the breath of his pride;
And the foam of his gasping lay white on the turf,
And cold as the spray of the rock-beating surf.

V

And there lay the rider distorted and pale,
With the dew on his brow, and the rust on his mail;
And the tents were all silent, the banners alone,
The lances unlifted, the trumpet unblown.

VI

And the widows of Ashur are loud in their wail,
And the idols are broke in the temple of Baal;
And the might of the Gentile, unsmote by the sword,
Hath melted like snow in the glance of the Lord.

GEORGE GORDON, LORD BYRON

THE TREES ARE DOWN

—and he cried with a
loud voice: Hurt not the
earth, neither the sea,
nor the trees—
(Revelation.)

They are cutting down the great plane-trees at the end of the gardens.
For days there has been the grate of the saw, the swish of the branches as
    they fall,
The crash of trunks, the rustle of trodden leaves,
With the "Whoops" and the "Whoas," and the loud common talk, the loud
    common laughs of the men, above it all.
I remember one evening of a long past Spring
Turning in at a gate, getting out of a cart, and finding a large dead rat in the
    mud of the drive.
I remember thinking: alive or dead, a rat was a god-forsaken thing,
But at least, in May, that even a rat should be alive.
The week's work here is as good as done. There is just one bough
  On the roped bole, in the fine grey rain.
    Green and high
    And lonely against the sky.
      (Down now!—)
    And but for that,
    If an old dead rat
Did once, for a moment, unmake the Spring, I might never have thought of
    him again.
It is not for a moment the Spring is unmade to-day;
These were great trees, it was in them from root to stem:
When the men with the "Whoops" and the "Whoas" have carted the whole
    of the whispering loveliness away
Half the Spring, for me, will have gone with them.
It is going now, and my heart has been struck with the hearts of the planes;
Half my life it has beat with these, in the sun, in the rains,
  In the March wind, the May breeze,
In the great gales that came over to them across the roofs from the great seas.

There was only a quiet rain when they were dying;
They must have heard the sparrows flying,
And the small creeping creatures in the earth where they were lying—
But I, all day, I heard an angel crying:
"Hurt not the trees."

CHARLOTTE MEW

Christian Community

EVE

Eve, with her basket, was
Deep in the bells and grass,
Wading in bells and grass
Up to her knees,
Picking a dish of sweet
Berries and plums to eat,
Down in the bells and grass
Under the trees.

Mute as a mouse in a
Corner the cobra lay,
Curled round a bough of the
Cinnamon tall. . . .
Now to get even and
Humble proud heaven and
Now was the moment or
Never at all.

"Eva!" Each syllable
Light as a flower fell;
"Eva!" he whispered the
Wondering maid;
Soft as a bubble sung
Out of a linnet's lung,
Soft and most silverly
"Eva!" he said.

Picture that orchard sprite,
Eve, with her body white,
Supple and smooth to her
Slim finger tips,
Wondering, listening,
Listening, wondering,
Eve with a berry
Half-way to her lips.

Oh, had our simple Eve
Seen through the make-believe!
Had she but known the
Pretender he was!
Out of the boughs he came,
Whispering still her name,
Tumbling in twenty rings
Into the grass.

Here was the strangest pair
In the world anywhere,
Eve in the bells and grass
Kneeling, and he
Telling his story low. . . .
Singing birds saw them go
Down the dark path to
The Blasphemous Tree.

Oh, what a clatter when
Titmouse and Jenny Wren
Saw him successful and
Taking his leave!
How the birds rated him,
How they all hated him!
How they all pitied
Poor motherless Eve!

Picture her crying
Outside in the lane,
Eve, with no dish of sweet
Berries and plums to eat,
Haunting the gate of the
Orchard in vain. . . .
Picture the lewd delight
Under the hill to-night—
"Eva!" the toast goes round,
"Eva!" again.

RALPH HODGSON

THE FOUR AGES OF MAN

He with body waged a fight,
But body won; it walks upright.

Then he struggled with the heart;
Innocence and peace depart.

Then he struggled with the mind;
His proud heart he left behind.

Now his wars on God begin;
At stroke of midnight God shall win.

WILLIAM BUTLER YEATS

THE RELAPSE

My God how gracious art Thou! I had slipt
    Almost to hell,
And on the verge of that dark, dreadful pit
    Did hear them yell,
But O Thy love, Thy rich, almighty love
    That saved my soul,
And checked their fury when I saw them move
    And heard them howl!
O my sole Comfort, take no more these ways,
    This hideous path,
And I will mend my own without delays.
    Cease Thou Thy wrath!
I have deserved a thick, Egyptian damp,
    Dark as my deeds,
Should mist within me and put out that lamp
    Thy Spirit feeds;
A darting conscience full of stabs and fears,
    No shade but yew.
Sullen and sad eclipses, cloudy spheres,
    These are my due.
But He that with His blood (a price too dear)
    My scores did pay
Bid me, by virtue from Him, challenge here
    The brightest day.
Sweet, downy thoughts, soft lily-shades, calm streams,
    Joys full and true,
Fresh, spicy mornings and eternal beams—
    These are His due.

HENRY VAUGHAN

MAN CANNOT NAME HIMSELF

Man cannot
name himself

He waits for God
or Satan
to tell him
who he is

LUCI SHAW

THE APPLE

Broken from the bursting bough
And bitten, they who searched it saw
The secret knowledge of their need,
Change at the core, the biding seed.
Diminished branch and ravished fruit
Forever troubling leaf and root.
Then legend placed a flaming sword
That none again might Edenward
Find in the shade of such a tree
The innocence of childhood's eye.

RAY SMITH

THE PURSUIT

Lord! what a busy, restless thing
    Hast thou made man?
Each day, and hour he is on wing,
    Rests not a span;
Then having lost the Sun, and light
    By clouds surpris'd
He keeps a Commerce in the night
    With air disguis'd;
Hadst thou given to this active dust
    A state untir'd,
The lost Son had not left the husk
    Nor home desir'd;
That was thy secret, and it is
    Thy mercy too,
For when all fails to bring to bliss,
    Then, this must do.
Ah! Lord! and what a Purchase will that be
To take us sick, that sound would not take thee?

HENRY VAUGHAN

INDIFFERENCE

When Jesus came to Golgotha they hanged Him on a tree,
They drave great nails through hands and feet, and made a Calvary;
They crowned Him with a crown of thorns, red were His wounds and deep,
For those were crude and cruel days, and human flesh was cheap.

When Jesus came to Birmingham, they simply passed Him by,
They never hurt a hair of Him, they only let Him die;
For men had grown more tender, and they would not give Him pain,
They only just passed down the street, and left Him in the rain.

Still Jesus cried, "Forgive them, for they know not what they do,"
And still it rained the wintry rain that drenched Him through and through;
The crowds went home and left the streets without a soul to see,
And Jesus crouched against a wall and cried for Calvary.

G. A. STUDDERT-KENNEDY

THE WINDOWS

Lord, how can man preach thy eternal Word?
   He is a brittle crazy glass:
Yet in thy temple thou dost him afford
   This glorious and transcendent place,
   To be a window, through thy grace.

But when thou dost anneal in glass thy story,
   Making thy life to shine within
The holy Preachers; then the light and glory
   More reverend grows, and more doth win;
   Which else shows waterish, bleak, and thin.

Doctrine and life, colors and light, in one
   When they combine and mingle, bring
A strong regard and awe: but speech alone
   Doth vanish like a flaring thing,
   And in the ear, not conscience ring.

GEORGE HERBERT

PAX

All that matters is to be at one with the
    living God
To be a creature in the house of the God of
    Life.
Like a cat asleep on a chair
At peace, in peace
And at one with the master of the house,
    with the mistress,
At home, at home in the house of the living,
Sleeping on the hearth, and yawning before
    the fire.

Sleeping on the hearth of the living world
Yawning at home before the fire of life
Feeling the presence of the living God
Like a great reassurance
A deep calm in the heart
A presence
As of the master sitting at the board
In his own and greater being,
In the house of life.

D. H. LAWRENCE

TWICE

I took my heart in my hand,
  (O my love, O my love),
I said: Let me fall or stand,
  Let me live or die,
But this once hear me speak
  (O my love, O my love)—
Yet a woman's words are weak;
  You should speak, not I.

You took my heart in your hand
  With a friendly smile,
With a critical eye you scann'd,
  Then set it down,
And said: 'It is still unripe,
  Better wait awhile;
Wait while the skylarks pipe,
  Till the corn grows brown.'

As you set it down it broke—
  Broke, but I did not wince;
I smiled at the speech you spoke,
  At your judgment I heard:
But I have not often smiled
  Since then, nor question'd since,
Nor cared for cornflowers wild,
  Nor sung with the singing bird.

I take my heart in my hand,
  O my God, O my God,
My broken heart in my hand:
  Thou hast seen, judge Thou.
My hope was written on sand,
  O my God, O my God:
Now let Thy judgment stand—
  Yea, judge me now.

This contemn'd of a man,
  This marr'd one heedless day,
This heart take Thou to scan
  Both within and without:
Refine with fire its gold,
  Purge Thou its dross away—
Yea, hold it in Thy hold,
  Whence none can pluck it out.

I take my heart in my hand—
  I shall not die, but live—
Before Thy face I stand;
  I, for Thou callest such:
All that I have I bring,
  All that I am I give,
Smile Thou and I shall sing,
  But shall not question much.

CHRISTINA ROSSETTI

THE NAKED SEED

My heart is empty. All the fountains that should run
      With longing, are in me
Dried up. In all my countryside there is not one
      That drips to find the sea.
I have no care for anything thy love can grant
      Except the moment's vain
And hardly noticed filling of the moment's want
      And to be free from pain.
Oh, thou that art unwearying, that dost neither sleep
      Nor slumber, who didst take
All care for Lazarus in the careless tomb, oh keep
      Watch for me till I wake.
If thou think for me what I cannot think, if thou
      Desire for me what I
Cannot desire, my soul's interior Form, though now
      Deep-buried, will not die,
—No more than the insensible dropp'd seed which grows
      Through winter ripe for birth
Because, while it forgets, the heaven remembering throws
      Sweet influence still on earth,
—Because the heaven, moved moth-like by thy beauty, goes
      Still turning round the earth.

C. S. LEWIS

THE PRAYER

Wilt thou not visit me?
The plant beside me feels thy gentle dew,
    And every blade of grass I see
From thy deep earth its quickening moisture drew.

Wilt Thou not visit me?
Thy morning calls on me with cheering tone;
    And every hill and tree
Lend but one voice,—the voice of thee alone.

Come, for I need thy love,
More than the flower the dew or grass the rain;
    Come, gently as thy holy dove;
And let me in thy sight rejoice to live again.

I will not hide from them,
When thy storms come, though fierce may be their wrath,
    But bow with leafy stem,
And strengthened follow on thy chosen path.

Yes, thou wilt visit me;
Nor plant nor tree thine eye delights so well,
    As when from sin set free,
My spirit loves with thine in peace to dwell.

JONES VERY

THE ALTAR

A broken ALTAR, Lord, thy servant rears,
Made of a heart, and cemented with tears:
  Whose parts are as thy hand did frame;
  No workman's tool hath touched the same.
      A   HEART   alone
      Is   such   a   stone,
      As   nothing   but
      Thy power doth cut.
      Wherefore each part
      Of my hard heart
      Meets in this frame,
      To praise thy Name:
  That, if I chance to hold my peace,
  These stones to praise thee may not cease.
Oh let thy blessed SACRIFICE be mine,
And sanctify this ALTAR to be thine.

GEORGE HERBERT

AM I THY GOLD?

Am I Thy gold? Or purse, Lord, for Thy wealth,
　　Whether in mine or mint refined for Thee?
I'm counted so, but count me o'er Thyself,
　　Lest gold-washed face and brass in heart I be.
　　I fear my Touchstone touches when I try
　　Me and my counted gold too overly.

Am I new minted by Thy stamp indeed?
　　Mine eyes are dim; I cannot clearly see.
Be Thou my spectacles that I may read
　　Thine image and inscription stamped on me.
　　If Thy bright image do upon me stand,
　　I am a golden angel in Thy hand.

Lord, make my soul Thy plate; Thine image bright
　　Within the circle of the same enfoil.
And on its brims in golden letters write
　　Thy superscription in an holy style.
　　Then I shall be Thy money, Thou my hoard;
　　Let me Thy angel be, be Thou my Lord.

EDWARD TAYLOR

PRAYER

Master, they say that when I seem
   To be in speech with you,
Since you make no replies, it's all a dream
   —One talker aping two.

They are half right, but not as they
   Imagine; rather, I
Seek in myself the things I meant to say,
   And lo! the wells are dry.

Then, seeing me empty, you forsake
   The Listener's role, and through
My dead lips breathe and into utterance wake
   The thoughts I never knew.

C. S. LEWIS

NEED IS OUR NAME

wide is our mouth and
our hands reach always
upward
need is our name

   Giving
   is Yours

we are machines
of no certain function
aching in all our axles
pain is our name

   Healing
   is Yours

we are in battle
between bombs we stumble
over the bodies
defeat is our name

   Triumph
   is Yours

LUCI SHAW

DAY BY DAY THE MANNA FELL

Day by day the manna fell;
Oh, to learn this lesson well!
Still, by constant mercy fed,
Give me, Lord, my daily bread.

"Day by day," the promise reads;
Daily strength for daily needs:
Cast foreboding fears away;
Take the manna of to-day.

Lord, my times are in Thy hand.
All my sanguine hopes have
        planned
To Thy wisdom I resign,
And would make Thy purpose
        mine.

Thou my daily task shalt give:
Day by day to Thee I live:
So shall added years fulfil,
Not my own,—my Father's will.

Fond ambition, whisper not;
Happy is my humble lot.
Anxious, busy cares, away;
I'm provided for to-day.

Oh, to live exempt from care
By the energy of prayer;
Strong in faith, with mind subdued,
Yet elate with gratitude.

JOSIAH CONDER

DOST THOU REMEMBER ME?

Saviour, I've no one else to tell
And so I trouble Thee,
I am the one forgot Thee so—
Dost Thou remember me?

Not, for myself I came so far,
That were the little load—

I brought Thee the imperial Heart
I had not strength to hold.

The heart I carried in my own—
Till mine too heavy be,
Yet strangest—*heavier*
Since it went—
Is it too large for Thee?

EMILY DICKINSON

A THANKSGIVING TO GOD

Lord, Thou hast given me a cell
      Wherein to dwell,
A little house, whose humble roof
      Is weather-proof;
Under the spars of which I lie
      Both soft and dry;
Where Thou, my chamber for to ward,
      Hast set a guard
Of harmless thoughts, to watch and keep
      Me while I sleep.
Low is my porch, as is my fate,
      Both void of state;
And yet the threshold of my door,
      Is worn by the poor,
Who thither come and freely get
      Good words or meat.
Like as my parlor, so my hall
      And kitchen's small;
A little buttery, and therein
      A little bin,
Which keeps my little loaf of bread
      Unchipped, unflead.
Some brittle sticks of thorn or brier
      Make me a fire,
Close by whose living coal I sit,
      And glow like it.
Lord I confess, too, when I dine
      The pulse is Thine,
And all those other bits that be
      There placed by Thee;
The worts, the purslane and the mess
      Of watercress,
Which of Thy kindness Thou hast sent;
      And my content

Makes those, and my beloved beet,
    To be more sweet.
'Tis Thou that crown'st my glittering hearth
    With guiltless mirth,
And givst me wassail bowls to drink,
    Spiced to the brink.
Lord 'tis Thy plenty-dropping hand
    That soils my land,
And givst me, for my bushel sown,
    Twice ten for one;
Thou makst my teeming hen to lay
    Her egg each day;
Besides my healthful ewes to bear
    Me twins each year;
The while the conduits of my kine
    Run cream for wine.

All these, and better, Thou dost send
    Me, to this end,
That I should render for my part
    A thankful heart;
Which, fired with incense, I resign
    As wholly Thine;
But the acceptance, that must be,
    My Christ, by thee.

ROBERT HERRICK

BE WITH ME, LORD

Be with me, Lord. Keep me beyond all prayers:
For more than all my prayers my need of thee,
And thou beyond all need, all unknown cares;
What the heart's dear imagination dares,
Thou dost transcend in measureless majesty
All prayers in one—my God, be unto me
Thy own eternal self, absolutely.

Be thou the well by which I lie and rest:
Be thou my tree of life, my garden ground;
Be thou my home, my fire, my chamber blest,
My book of wisdom, loved of all the best;
Oh, be my friend, each day still newer found,
As the eternal days and nights go round!
Nay, nay—thou art *my* God, in whom all loves are bound!

Thou workest perfectly. And if it seem
Some things are not so well, 'tis but because
They are too loving-deep, too lofty-wise,
For me, poor child, to understand their laws:
My highest wisdom half is but a dream;
My love runs helpless like a falling stream;
Thy good embraces ill, and lo, its illness dies!

GEORGE MACDONALD
From *Diary of an Old Soul*

EVERYMAID

King's Daughter!
Wouldst thou be all fair,
Without—within—
Peerless and beautiful,
A very Queen?

Know then:—
Not as men build unto the Silent One,—
With clang and clamour,
Traffic of rude voices,
Clink of steel on stone,
And din of hammer;—
Not so the temple of thy grace is reared.
But,—in the inmost shrine
Must thou begin,
And build with care
A Holy Place,
A place unseen,
Each stone a prayer.
Then, having built,
Thy shrine sweep bare
Of self and sin,
And all that might demean;
And, with endeavour,
Watching ever, praying ever,
Keep it fragrant-sweet, and clean:
So, by God's grace, it be fit place,—
His Christ shall enter and shall dwell therein.
Not as in earthly fane—where chase
Of steel on stone may strive to win
Some outward grace,—
Thy temple face is chiselled from within.

JOHN OXENHAM

140

SEEK THE LORD!

Seek the Lord, and in His ways persever.
    O faint not, but as eagles fly;
    For His steep hill is high;
Then striving gain the top, and triumph ever.

When with glory there thy brows are crowned,
    New joys so shall abound in thee,
    Such sights thy soul shall see,
That worldly thoughts shall by their beams be drowned.

Farewell, World, thou mass of mere confusion,
    False light, with many shadows dimmed,
    Old Witch, with new foils trimmed,
Thou deadly sleep of soul, and charmed illusion.

I the King will seek, of kings adored;
    Spring of light, tree of grace and bliss,
    Whose fruit so sovereign is
That all who taste it are from death restored.

THOMAS CAMPION

TO KEEP A TRUE LENT

Is this a fast, to keep
    The larder lean,
        And clean
From fat of veals and sheep?

Is it to quit the dish
    Of flesh, yet still
        To fill
The platter high with fish?

Is it to fast an hour,
    Or ragg'd to go,
        Or show
A downcast look and sour?

No: 'tis a Fast to dole
    Thy sheaf of wheat
        And meat,
Unto the hungry soul.

It is to fast from strife,
    From old debate
        And hate;
To circumcise thy life.

To show a heart grief-rent;
    To starve thy sin,
        Not bin:
And that's to keep thy Lent.

ROBERT HERRICK

INVOCATION

Great-hearted Christ, importunate and mild,
 Whose time was time enough for woman and well,
Whose arms were slow enough for any child,
 And made the necessary trip to hell,
Fate-parted Christ, why did you leave me so?
 In bread and wine and bed and vine I see you
And in the small gnats when the sun is low
 And in the darkness too. They cannot be you,
Not all can be. Late-started Christ, return;
 Be in a certain time and public place.
If they can see you once, my eyes will learn
 To see you under any other face
You wear, and if all faces are your own
And places, then I worship you alone.

CHAD WALSH
From *The Psalm of Christ*

JORDAN (I)

Who says that fictions only and false hair
Become a verse? Is there in truth no beauty?
Is all good structure in a winding stair?
May no lines pass, except they do their duty
 Not to a true, but painted chair?

Is it no verse, except enchanted groves
And sudden arbors shadow coarse-spun lines?
Must purling streams refresh a lover's loves?
Must all be veiled while he that reads, divines,
 Catching the sense at two removes?

Shepherds are honest people; let them sing:
Riddle who list, for me, and pull for prime:
I envy no man's nightingale or spring;
Nor let them punish me with loss of rhyme,
 Who plainly say, *My God, My King.*

GEORGE HERBERT

WHAT RIDER SPURS HIM FROM
THE DARKENING EAST

What rider spurs him from the darkening east
As from a forest, and with rapid pound
Of hooves, now light, now louder on hard ground,
Approaches, and rides past with speed increased,
Dark spots and flecks of foam upon his beast?
What shouts he from the saddle, turning 'round
As he rides on?—"Greetings!"—I made the sound;
"Greetings from Nineveh!"—it seemed, at least.
Did someone catch the object that he flung?
He held some object on his saddle-bow,
And flung it towards us as he passed; among
The children then it fell most likely; no,
'Tis here: a little bell without a tongue.
Listen; it has a faint voice even so.

EDNA ST. VINCENT MILLAY

I LOVE ALL BEAUTEOUS THINGS

I love all beauteous things,
　I seek and adore them;
God hath no better praise,
And man in his hasty days
　Is honored for them.

I too will something make
　And joy in the making;
Although to-morrow it seem
Like the empty words of a dream
　Remembered on waking.

ROBERT BRIDGES

143

SWIFTLY AROSE

Swiftly arose and spread around me the peace and knowledge
      that pass all the argument of the earth,
And I know that the hand of God is the promise of my own,
And I know that the spirit of God is the brother of my own,
And that all the men ever born are also my brothers, and the
      women my sisters and lovers,
And that a kelson of the creation is love,
And limitless are leaves stiff or drooping in the fields,
And brown ants in the little wells beneath them,
And mossy scabs of the worm fence, heap'd stones, elder,
      mullein and poke-weed.

WALT WHITMAN
From *Song of Myself*

ON FINDING THE TRUTH

With sweet surprise, as when one finds a flower,
Which in some lonely spot unheeded grows;
Such were my feelings, in the favored hour
When Truth to me her beauty did disclose.
Quickened, I gazed anew on heaven and earth,
For a new glory beamed from earth and sky;
All things around me shared the second birth,
Restored with me, and nevermore to die.
The happy habitants of other spheres,
As in times past, from heaven to earth came down;
Swift fled in converse sweet the unnumbered years,
And angel-help did human weakness crown!
The former things, with Time, had passed away,
And Man and Nature lived again for aye.

JONES VERY

LAUDS

Among the leaves the small birds sing;
The crow of the cock commands awaking:
In solitude, for company.

Bright shines the sun on creatures mortal;
Men of their neighbours become sensible:
In solitude, for company.

The crow of the cock commands awaking;
Already the mass-bell goes dong-ding:
In solitude, for company.

Men of their neighbours become sensible;
God bless the Realm, God bless the People:
In solitude, for company.

Already the mass-bell goes dong-ding;
The dripping mill-wheel is again turning:
In solitude, for company.

God bless the Realm, God bless the People;
God bless this green world temporal:
In solitude, for company.

The dripping mill-wheel is again turning;
Among the leaves the small birds sing:
In solitude, for company.

W. H. AUDEN

THE GARDENER TO HIS GOD

"Amazing research proves simple prayer makes flowers grow many times
faster, stronger, larger."
—*Advertisement in* The Flower Grower

I pray that the great world's flowering stay as it is,
that larkspur and snapdragon keep to their ordinary size,
and bleedingheart hang in its old way, and Judas tree
stand well below oak, and old oaks color the fall sky.
For the myrtle to keep underfoot, and no rose
to send up a swollen face, I pray simply.

There is no disorder but the heart's. But if love goes leaking
outward, if shrubs take up its monstrous stalking,
all greenery is spurred, the snapping lips are overgrown,
and over oaks red hearts hang like the sun.
Deliver us from its giant gardening, from walking
all over the earth with no rest from its disproportion.

Let all flowers turn to stone before ever they begin to share
love's spaciousness, and faster, stronger, larger
grow from a sweet thought, before any daisy
turns, under love's gibberellic wish, to the day's eye.
Let all blooms take shape from cold laws, down from a cold air
let come their small grace or measurable majesty.

For in every place but love the imagination lies
in its limits. Even poems draw back from images
of that one country, on top of whose lunatic stemming
whoever finds himself there must sway and cling
until the high cold God takes pity, and it all dies
down, down into the great world's flowering.

MONA VAN DUYN

RETURN TO ARARAT

The rainbow faded, the animals dispersed,
Seeking new dens, new haunts after the flood;
The family stayed awhile, though fidgeting
For a new farm; only Noah being loath to leave.

Each day he checked the present stock on board,
Calling each creature, clambering to the eaves
And the great thatch thick with nesting, commenting
Over supper later: 'That camel's foaled, you know.
Those young owls will be flying soon and then
The mice will catch it; did I tell you that . . .'
Noah's wife said, 'Come on husband, eat your fish,
We're not a naval family, let's go home.'

Even as they moved downhill, the donkeys laden,
Dogs and cats with them, cattle tethered, poultry crated,
The old man slowed his step. 'Quite a boat,' he said
Looking back, 'quite a boat for a farmer and
Quite a stock for a hundred acre man;
Thank you, Lord, for the dimensions.'

They settled in the plain, alluvial soil
Ensuring heavy crops, the families prospered,
Only the old man doing very much with stock:
'I like the beasts,' he said, 'they keep me young.'

And after several years a straying bullock
Brought him again to the slopes, now dry, now growing
Thick underfoot, he rose, by talking streams,
Land between trees cobbled with good granite, purple heather.

Noah strode on upwards, his staff sparking rough rock,
Grass and plant, after their kind, seeding his robe;
Height, like the breeze, sweeping the years away—
Over a crest the ark lay wedged on the peak.

Worshiping he entered; inside lion and lamb
Lay down together, tiger and stumbling calf;
Over his head light poured through thinning thatch,
Birds of all kinds forested their chorus:
'This was your mountain, Lord, and holy still,'
And his tears were thicker than forty days of rain.

MARTYN HALSALL

A LOST WORD OF JESUS

Hear the word that Jesus spake
  Eighteen centuries ago,
  Where the crimson lilies blow
Round the blue Tiberian lake:
There the bread of Life he brake,
  Through the fields of harvest walking
  With his lowly comrades, talking
Of the secret thoughts that feed
Weary hearts in time of need.
  Art thou hungry? Come and take;
  Hear the word that Jesus spake.
'Tis the sacrament of labor; meat and drink divinely blest,
Friendship's food, and sweet refreshment; strength and courage, joy and
    rest.

Yet this word the Master said,
  Long ago and far away,
  Silent and forgotten lay
Buried with the silent dead,—
Where the sands of Egypt spread,
  Sea-like, tawny billows heaping
  Over ancient cities sleeping;
While the river Nile between
Rolls its summer floods of green,
  Rolls its autumn flood of red,—
  There the word the Master said
Written on a frail papyrus, scorched by fire, wrinkled, torn,
Hidden in God's hand, was waiting for its resurrection morn.

Hear the Master's risen word!
   Delving spades have set it free,—
   Wake! the world has need of thee,—
Rise, and let thy voice be heard,
Like a fountain disinterred.
   Upward-springing, singing, sparkling;
   Through the doubtful shadows darkling;
Till the clouds of pain and rage
Brooding, o'er the toiling age,
   As with rifts of light are stirred
   By the music of the word;
Gospel for the heavy-laden, answer to the labourer's cry;
"Raise the stone and thou shalt find me; cleave the wood, and
    there am I."

HENRY VAN DYKE

LORD, HEAR MY PRAYER
A Paraphrase of the 102nd Psalm

Lord, hear my prayer when trouble glooms,
Let sorrow find a way,
And when the day of trouble comes,
Turn not thy face way:
My bones like hearthstones burn away,
My life like vapory smoke decays.

My heart is smitten like the grass,
That withered lies and dead,
And I, so lost to what I was,
Forget to eat my bread.
My voice is groaning all the day,
My bones prick through this skin of clay.

The wilderness's pelican,
The desert's lonely owl—
I am their like, a desert man
In ways as lone and foul.
As sparrows on the cottage top
I wait till I with fainting drop.

I hear my enemies reproach,
All silently I mourn;
They on my private peace encroach,
Against me they are sworn.
Ashes as bread my trouble shares,
And mix my food with weeping cares.

Yet not for them is sorrow's toil,
I fear no mortal's frowns—
But thou hast held me up awhile
And thou hast cast me down.
My days like shadows waste from view,
I mourn like withered grass in dew.

But thou, Lord, shalt endure for ever,
All generations through;
Thou shalt to Zion be the giver
Of joy and mercy too.
Her very stones are in thy trust,
Thy servants reverence her dust.

Heathens shall hear and fear thy name,
All kings of earth thy glory know
When thou shalt build up Zion's fame
And live in glory there below.
He'll not despise their prayers, though mute,
But still regard the destitute.

JOHN CLARE

THE APOLOGIST'S EVENING PRAYER

From all my lame defeats and oh! much more
From all the victories that I seemed to score;
From cleverness shot forth on Thy behalf
At which, while angels weep, the audience laugh;
From all my proofs of Thy divinity,
Thou, who wouldst give no sign, deliver me.

Thoughts are but coins. Let me not trust, instead
Of Thee, their thin-worn image of Thy head.
From all my thoughts, even from my thoughts of Thee,
O thou fair Silence, fall, and set me free.
Lord of the narrow gate and the needle's eye,
Take from me all my trumpery lest I die.

C. S. LEWIS

IF ONLY

If I might only love my God and die!
But now He bids me love Him and live on,
Now when the bloom of all my life is gone,
The pleasant half of life has quite gone by.
My tree of hope is lopped that spread so high;
And I forget how summer glowed and shone,
While autumn grips me with its fingers wan,
And frets me with its fitful windy sigh.
When autumn passes, then must winter numb,
And winter may not pass a weary while,
But when it passes, spring shall flower again:
And in that spring who weepeth now shall smile;
Yea, they shall wax who now are on the wane—
Yea, they shall sing for love when Christ shall come.

CHRISTINA ROSSETTI

WHEN I CONSIDER HOW MY LIGHT IS SPENT

When I consider how my light is spent
 Ere half my days, in this dark world and wide,
 And that one talent which is death to hide,
 Lodged with me useless, though my soul more bent
To serve therewith my Maker, and present
 My true account, lest he returning chide;
 "Doth God exact day-labor, light denied?"
 I fondly ask; but Patience to prevent
That murmur soon replies, "God doth not need
 Either man's work or his own gifts; who best
 Bear his mild yoke, they serve him best. His state
Is kingly. Thousands at his bidding speed
 And post o'er land and ocean without rest:
 They also serve who only stand and wait."

JOHN MILTON

HOLY SONNET 14

Batter my heart, three-personed God; for You
As yet but knock, breathe, shine, and seek to mend;
That I may rise and stand, o'erthrow me, and bend
Your force to break, blow, burn, and make me new.
I, like an usurped town, to another due,
Labor to admit You, but O, to no end;
Reason, Your viceroy in me, me should defend,
But is captived, and proves weak or untrue.
Yet dearly I love You, and would be loved fain,
But am betrothed unto Your enemy.
Divorce me, untie or break that knot again;
Take me to You, imprison me, for I,
Except You enthrall me, never shall be free,
Nor ever chaste, except You ravish me.

JOHN DONNE

SONNET XV

But we are set to strive to make our mark
And scarcely pause to plead for any play
Nor think that any hour of any day
Writes its own record down in chalk or chark,
For all we falsely claim or blindly say,
"I am the Truth, the Life too and the Way."
It stands, a word to comfort and appal,
A summons grave and sweet, a warning stark.
But death and dread responsibility
I hardly fear tonight, or feel at all:
Watching my fancy gleam, now bright, now dark,
As snapping from the brands a single spark
Splits in a spray of sparkles ere it fall,
And the long flurrying flame that shoots to die. . . .

FREDERICK GODDARD TUCKERMAN

CREDO

I cannot find my way: there is no star
In all the shrouded heavens anywhere;
And there is not a whisper in the air
Of any living voice but one so far
That I can hear it only as a bar
Of lost, imperial music, played when fair
And angel fingers wove, and unaware,
Dead leaves to garlands where no roses are.

No, there is not a glimmer, nor a call,
For one that welcomes, welcomes when he fears,
The black and awful chaos of the night;
For through it all—above, beyond it all—
I know the far-sent message of the years,
I feel the coming glory of the Light.

EDWARD ARLINGTON ROBINSON

UP-HILL

Does the road wind up-hill all the way?
   Yes, to the very end.
Will the day's journey take the whole long day?
   From morn to night, my friend.

But is there for the night a resting-place?
   A roof for when the slow dark hours begin.
May not the darkness hide it from my face?
   You cannot miss that inn.

Shall I meet other wayfarers at night?
   Those who have gone before.
Then must I knock, or call when just in sight?
   They will not keep you standing at that door.

Shall I find comfort, travel-sore and weak?
   Of labour you shall find the sum.
Will there be beds for me and all who seek?
   Yea, beds for all who come.

CHRISTINA ROSSETTI

PILGRIM'S PROBLEM

By now I should be entering on the supreme stage
Of the whole walk, reserved for the late afternoon.
The heat was to be over now; the anxious mountains,
The airless valleys and the sun-baked rocks, behind me.

Now, or soon now, if all is well, come the majestic
Rivers of foamless charity that glide beneath
Forests of contemplation. In the grassy clearings
Humility with liquid eyes and damp, cool nose
Should come, half-tame, to eat bread from my hermit hand.
If storms arose, then in my tower of fortitude—

It ought to have been in sight by this—I would take refuge;
But I expected rather a pale mackerel sky,
Feather-like, perhaps shaking from a lower cloud
Light drops of silver temperance, and clovery earth
Sending up mists of chastity, a country smell,
Till earnest stars blaze out in the established sky
Rigid with justice; the streams audible; my rest secure.

I can see nothing like all this. Was the map wrong?
Maps can be wrong. But the experienced walker knows
That the other explanation is more often true.

C. S. LEWIS

WRITTEN IN EXILE

There is a word at heart for the next of death,
The farthest from joy; if I could fathom it
I would from this most desolate and distant place, bless

The maker of distances, since what divides
Me from His presence is the extent of Heaven.
Were He less high, I could not be so far.

And my unrest fathoms the deep of peace,
And by my depth downcast, Lord, You are risen,
Your love's great realm, my separation measures.

KATHLEEN RAINE

THE FIRE BURNS LOW

Issues from the hand of time the simple soul
Irresolute and selfish, misshapen, lame
Unable to face forward or retreat . . .
—T. S. Eliot "Animula"

Thursday evening

Inside the light of a three-way lamp
he sits absorbed
reading
the living word reduced
to monosyllables,
the gospel cut like hash
for middleclass consumption

He does not like abstractions;
he takes the words as they come,
nouns, verbs, and articles.
They move him, but he does not
move.
Each verse, each phrase
he reads reminds him
he died with Christ in 1963.
He remembers the day,
moistens his lips and begins to
recite
"I am dead . . ."
but he can't remember the rest.
He mortifies the flesh; his right
leg prickles asleep.

Thursday night

In the dark he loves his wife
not well or long (the hour is late)
but moderately, discreetly
as Christ will woo the church.

Friday morning

The desk he works at is as clean
as his mind,
Nothing piles up into confusion.
He is praised but not promoted.

Sunday morning

In church he waits on the Lord
and is never disappointed.

Sunday afternoon

After the roast and baked potatoes
occasionally with a dab
of sour cream,
he settles in front of the sleep
machine
and watches time run out
on the Baltimore Colts.
That disappoints him; he'd like his
son
to worship Johnny U
but Namath gets the girls
and postgame interview.

Sunday evening

The evening meal is never much—
leftovers, eggs,
maybe a piece of chocolate cake
with ice cream
then back to church
for one more admonition
to catch fire for Jesus.

Bent over the kitchen table
he has no history.
The ceiling light shapes his head
on the page he reads.
From the shadow the living word
makes small talk with his soul.
He takes the words as they come,
he does not argue; the fire burns
low.
He relives again the day he died. . . .

JOHN LEAX

SENSITIVENESS

Time was, I shrank from what was right
    From fear of what was wrong;
I would not brave the sacred fight,
    Because the foe was strong.

But now I cast that finer sense
    And sorer shame aside;
Such dread of sin was indolence,
    Such aim at Heaven was pride.

So, when my Saviour calls, I rise
    And calmly do my best;
Leaving to Him, with silent eyes
    Of hope and fear, the rest.

I step, I mount where He has led;
    Men count my haltings o'er—
I know them; yet, though self I dread,
    I love His precept more.

JOHN HENRY NEWMAN

PRAYERS OF STEEL

Lay me on an anvil, O God.
Beat me and hammer me into a crowbar.
Let me pry loose old walls.
Let me lift and loosen old foundations.

Lay me on an anvil, O God.
Beat me and hammer me into a steel spike.
Drive me into the girders that hold a skyscraper together.
Take red-hot rivets and fasten me into the central girders.
Let me be the great nail holding a skyscraper through
            blue nights into white stars.

CARL SANDBURG

OLD-TESTAMENT GOSPEL

Israel in ancient days,
Not only had a view
Of Sinai in a blaze,
But learned the Gospel too;
The types and figures were a glass
In which they saw the Savior's face.

The paschal sacrifice
And blood-besprinkled door
Seen with enlightened eyes
And once applied with power
Would teach the need of other blood
To reconcile an angry God.

The Lamb, the Dove, set forth
His perfect innocence,
Whose blood, of matchless worth,
Should be the soul's defence;
For He who can for sin atone
Must have no failings of His own.

The scape-goat on his head
The people's trespass bore,
And to the desert led,
Was to be seen no more.
In him, our Surety seemed to say,
"Behold, I bear your sins away."

Dipped in his fellow's blood,
The living bird went free;
The type, well understood,
Expressed the sinner's plea,
Described a guilty soul enlarged
And by a Savior's death discharged.

Jesus, I love to trace
Throughout the sacred page
The footsteps of Thy grace,
The same in every age!
Oh grant that I may faithful be
To clearer light vouchsafed to me!

WILLIAM COWPER

A SOLILOQUY OF ONE OF THE SPIES LEFT IN THE WILDERNESS

Who is this Moses? who made him, we say,
To be a judge and ruler over us?
He slew the Egyptian yesterday. To-day
   In hot sands perilous
He hides our corpses dropping by the way
   Wherein he makes us stray.

Your hands have borne the tent-poles: on you plod:
The trumpet waxes loud: tired are your feet.
Come by the flesh-pots: you shall sit unshod
   And break your pleasant meat,
And bring your offerings to a grateful god,
   And fear no iron rod.

He feeds me with his manna every day:
My soul does loathe it and my spirit fails.
A press of wingéd things comes down this way:
   The gross flock call them quails.
Into my hand he gives a host for prey,
   Come up, Arise and slay.

Sicken'd and thicken'd by the glare of sand
Who would drink water from a stony rock?
Are all the manna-bushes in the land
   A shelter for this flock?
Behold at Elim wells on every hand
   And seventy palms there stand.

Egypt, the valley of our pleasance, there!
Most wide ye are who call this gust Simoom.
Your parchèd nostrils snuff Egyptian air,
    The comfortable gloom
After the sandfield and the unveinèd glare!
    Goshen is green and fair.

Not Goshen. Wasteful wide huge-girthèd Nile
Unbakes my pores, and streams, and makes all fresh.
I gather points of lote-flower from an isle
    Of leaves of greenest flesh.
Are you sandblind? slabs of water many a mile
    Blaze for him all this while.

In beds, in gardens, in thick plots I stand,
Handle the fig, suck the full-sapp'd vine-shoot.
From easy runnels the rich-piecèd land
    I water with my foot.
Must you be gorged with proof? Did ever sand
    So trickle from your hand?

Strike timbrels, sing, eat, drink, be full of mirth.
Forget the waking trumpet, the long law.
Spread o'er the swart face of this prodigal earth.
    Not manna bring, but straw.
Here are sweet messes without price or worth,
    And never thirst or dearth.

Give us the tale of bricks as heretofore;
To knead with cool feet the clay juicy soil.
Who tread the grapes are splay'd with stripes of gore,
    And they who crush the oil
Are spatter'd. We desire the yoke we bore,
    The easy burden of yore.

Go then: I am contented here to lie.
Take Canaan with your sword and with your bow.
Rise: match your strength with monstrous Talmai
    At Kirjath-Arba: go.—
Sure, this is Nile: I sicken, I know not why,
    And faint as though to die.

GERARD MANLEY HOPKINS

160

SAINT JOHN THE BAPTIST

The last and greatest Herald of Heaven's King,
Girt with rough skins, hies to the deserts wild,
Among that savage brood the woods forth bring,
Which he than man more harmless found and mild.
His food was locusts, and what young doth spring
With honey that from virgin hives distill'd;
Parch'd body, hollow eyes, some uncouth thing
Made him appear, long since from earth exiled.
There burst he forth: "All ye whose hopes rely
On God, with me amidst these deserts mourn;
Repent, repent, and from old errors turn."
—Who listened to his voice, obey'd his cry?
  Only the echoes which he made relent,
  Rung from their marble caves, "Repent, repent."

WILLIAM DRUMMOND

HOLY THURSDAY

'Twas on a Holy Thursday, their innocent faces clean,
The children walking two & two, in red & blue & green,
Grey-headed beadles walkd before with wands as white as snow,
Till into the high dome of Paul's they like Thames' waters flow.

O what a multitude they seemd, these flowers of London town!
Seated in companies they sit with radiance all their own.
The hum of multitudes was there, but multitudes of lambs,
Thousands of little boys & girls raising their innocent hands.

Now like a mighty wind they raise to heaven the voice of song,
Or like harmonious thunderings the seats of heaven among.
Beneath them sit the aged men, wise guardians of the poor;
Then cherish pity, lest you drive an angel from your door.

WILLIAM BLAKE

161

ALL IS VANITY, SAITH THE PREACHER

Fame, wisdom, love, and power were mine,
   And health and youth possess'd me;
My goblets blush'd from every vine,
   And lovely forms caress'd me;
I sunn'd my heart in beauty's eyes,
   And felt my soul grow tender;
All earth can give, or mortal prize,
   Was mine of regal splendour.

I strive to number o'er what days
   Remembrance can discover,
Which all that life or earth displays
   Would lure me to live over.
There rose no day, there roll'd no hour
   Of pleasure unembitter'd;
And not a trapping deck'd my power
   That gall'd not while it glitter'd.

The serpent of the field, by art
   And spells, is won from harming;
But that which coils around the heart,
   Oh! who hath power of charming?
It will not list to wisdom's lore,
   Nor music's voice can lure it;
But there it stings for evermore
   The soul that must endure it.

GEORGE GORDON, LORD BYRON

162

SUPPLICATION

For He knoweth our frame, He remembereth
    that we are dust.—Psalm ciii, 14

Oh Lord, when all our bones are thrust
    Beyond the gaze of all but Thine;
And these blaspheming tongues are dust
    Which babbled of Thy name divine,
How helpless then to carp or rail
    Against the canons of Thy word;
Wilt Thou, when thus our spirits fail,
    Have mercy, Lord?

Here from this ebon speck that floats
    As but a mote within Thine eye,
Vain sneers and curses from our throats
    Rise to the vault of Thy fair sky:
Yet when this world of ours is still
    Of this all-wondering, tortured horde,
And none is left for Thee to kill—
    Have mercy, Lord!

Thou knowest that our flesh is grass;
    Ah! let our withered souls remain
Like stricken reeds of some morass,
    Bleached, in Thy will, by ceaseless rain.
Have we not had enough of fire,
    Enough of torment and the sword?—
If these accrue from Thy desire—
    Have mercy, Lord!

Dost Thou not see about our feet
    The tangles of our erring thought?
Thou knowest that we run to greet
    High hopes that vanish into naught.
We bleed, we fall, we rise again;
    How can we be of Thee abhorred?
We are Thy breed, we little men—
    Have mercy, Lord!

Wilt Thou then slay for that we slay,
  Wilt Thou deny when we deny?
A thousand years are but a day,
  A little day within Thine eye:
We thirst for love, we yearn for life;
  We lust, wilt Thou the lust record?
We, beaten, fall upon the knife—
  Have mercy, Lord!

Thou givest us youth that turns to age;
  And strength that leaves us while we seek.
Thou pourest the fire of sacred rage
  In costly vessels all too weak.
Great works we planned in hopes that Thou
  Fit wisdom therefor wouldst accord;
Thou wrotest failure on our brow—
  Have mercy, Lord!

EDGAR LEE MASTERS

EVENSONG

Now that night is creeping
O'er our travail'd senses,
To Thy care unsleeping
We commit our sleep.
Nature for a season
Conquers our defences,
But th' eternal Reason
Watch and ward will keep.

All the soul we render
Back to Thee completely,
Trusting Thou wilt tend her
Through the deathlike hours,

And all night remake her
To Thy likeness sweetly,
Then with dawn awake her
And give back her powers.

Slumber's less uncertain
Brother soon will bind us
—Darker falls the curtain,
Stifling-close 'tis drawn:
But amidst that prison
Still Thy voice can find us,
And, as Thou hast risen,
Raise us in Thy dawn.

C. S. LEWIS

IN NO STRANGE LAND

O world invisible, we view thee,
O world intangible, we touch thee,
O world unknowable, we know thee,
Inapprehensible, we clutch thee!

Does the fish soar to find the ocean,
The eagle plunge to find the air—
That we ask of the stars in motion
If they have rumor of thee there?

Not where the wheeling systems darken
And our benumbed conceiving soars!—
The drift of pinions, would we hearken,
Beats at our own clay-shuttered doors.

The angels keep their ancient places—
Turn but a stone and start a wing!
'Tis ye, 'tis your estrangéd faces,
That miss the many-splendored thing.

But (when so sad thou canst not sadder)
Cry—and upon thy so sore loss
Shall shine the traffic of Jacob's ladder
Pitched betwixt Heaven and Charing Cross.

Yea, in the night, my Soul, my daughter,
Cry—clinging Heaven by the hems;
And lo, Christ walking on the water
Not of Genesareth, but Thames!

FRANCIS THOMPSON

LIFT UP YOUR HEADS, REJOICE

Lift up your heads, rejoice,
  Redemption draweth nigh!
Now breathes a softer air,
  Now shines a milder sky;
The early trees put forth
  Their new and tender leaf;
Hushed is the moaning wind
  That told of winter's grief.

Lift up your heads, rejoice,
  Redemption draweth nigh!
Now mount the leaden clouds,
  Now flames the darkening sky;
The early scattered drops
  Descend with heavy fall,
And to the waiting earth
  The hidden thunders call.

Lift up your heads, rejoice,
  Redemption draweth nigh!
O note the varying signs
  Of earth, and air, and sky;
The God of Glory comes
  In gentleness and might,
To comfort and alarm,
  To succour and to smite.

He comes the wide world's King,
  He comes the true heart's Friend,
New gladness to begin,
  And ancient wrong to end;
He comes, to fill with light
  The weary, waiting eye:
Lift up your heads, rejoice,
  Redemption draweth nigh.

THOMAS TOKE LYNCH

Μή λυπείται κανείς
Ο Σωτήρ ήλθ', Αυτός
Μέσ'στη Φάτνη γεννήθει
Και ο Χριστός
Και ζωή έστω Αυτόν
Και λατρεία τιμή
Δέξαρχα τον Πατέρα
μ' τον Χριστό
Μέσ' στη Φάτνη γεννήθει
τον Λυπηταί.

Χαρά, χαρά, Χριστούγεννα
Χαρήτε όλοι γεννήθει Χριστός.

Ε π ω θ ό ς

Νύχτα είναι γλυκειά
κι άνοιξε Ουρανός φάλλουν
Οι άγγελοι όλοι του Χριστός
γεννήθη ο Χριστός
Εδώ κάτω στη γη
Μάστ', αγαπημένε
Ναι, σως και αγάπη
του Θεός και σε.

-8-

Life Everlasting

NOAH'S PRAYER

Lord,
what a menagerie!
Between Your downpour and these animal cries
one cannot hear oneself think!
The days are long,
Lord.
All this water makes my heart sink.
When will the ground cease to rock under my feet?
The days are long.
Master Raven has not come back.
Here is Your dove.
Will she find us a twig of hope?
The days are long,
Lord.
Guide Your Ark to safety,
some zenith of rest,
where we can escape at last
from this brute slavery.
The days are long,
Lord.
Lead me until I reach the shore of Your covenant.

Amen

CARMEN BERNOS DE GASTOLD
Translated by Rumer Godden

WHERE LIES THE TRUTH? HAS MAN,
IN WISDOM'S CREED

Where lies the truth? has Man, in wisdom's creed,
A pitiable doom; for respite brief
A care more anxious, or a heavier grief?
Is he ungrateful, and doth little heed
God's bounty, soon forgotten; or indeed,
Must Man, with labour born, awake to sorrow
When Flowers rejoice and Larks with rival speed
Spring from their nests to bid the Sun good morrow?
They mount for rapture as their songs proclaim
Warbled in hearing both of earth and sky;
But o'er the contrast wherefore heave a sigh?
Like those aspirants let us soar—our aim,
Through life's worst trials, whether shocks or snares,
A happier, brighter, purer Heaven than theirs.

WILLIAM WORDSWORTH

IN MEMORY OF MY DEAR GRANDCHILD
Who Deceased June 20, 1669,
Being Three Years and Seven Months Old

With troubled heart and trembling hand I write,
The heavens have changed to sorrow my delight.
How oft with disappointment have I met,
When I on fading things my hopes have set.
Experience might 'fore this have made me wise,
To value things according to their price.
Was ever stable joy yet found below?
Or perfect bliss without mixture of woe?
I knew she was but as a withering flower,
That's here today, perhaps gone in an hour;
Like as a bubble, or the brittle glass,
Or like a shadow turning as it was.
More fool then I to look on that was lent
As if mine own, when thus impermanent.
Farewell dear child, thou ne'er shall come to me,
But yet a while, and I shall go to thee;
Meantime my throbbing heart's cheered up with this:
Thou with thy Savior art in endless bliss.

ANNE BRADSTREET

THE TWO MYSTERIES

We know not what it is, dear, this sleep so deep and still;
The folded hands, the awful calm, the cheek so pale and chill;
The lids that will not lift again, though we may call and call;
The strange white solitude of peace that settles over all.

We know not what it means, dear, this desolate heart pain;
This dread to take our daily way, and walk in it again;
We know not to what other sphere the loved who leave us go,
Nor why we're left to wonder still, nor why we do not know.

But this we know: our loved and dead, if they should come this day,—
Should come and ask us, "What is life?"—not one of us could say.
Life is a mystery, as deep as ever death can be;
Yet, oh, how dear it is to us, this life we live and see!

Then might they say—these vanished ones—and blessed is the thought,
"So death is sweet to us, beloved! though we may show you naught;
We may not to the quick reveal the mystery of death—
Ye cannot tell us, if ye would, the mystery of breath!"

The child who enters life comes not with knowledge or intent,
So those who enter death must go as little children sent.
Nothing is known. But I believe that God is overhead;
And as life is to the living, so death is to the dead.

MARY MAPES DODGE

THE WORLD

I saw eternity the other night
Like a great ring of pure and endless light,
    All calm as it was bright;
And round beneath it, Time, in hours, days, years,
        Driven by the spheres,
Like a vast shadow moved, in which the world
    And all her train were hurled:
The doting lover in his quaintest strain
        Did there complain;
Near him, his lute, his fancy, and his flights,
        Wit's sour delights,
With gloves and knots, the silly snares of pleasure,
        Yet his dear treasure,
All scattered lay, while he his eyes did pore
        Upon a flower.

The darksome statesman, hung with weights and woe,
Like a thick midnight fog moved there so slow
    He did not stay nor go;
Condemning thoughts, like sad eclipses, scowl
        Upon his soul,
And clouds of crying witnesses without
    Pursued him with one shout.
Yet digged the mole, and lest his ways be found,
        Worked underground,
Where he did clutch his prey. But One did see
        That policy:
Churches and altars fed him; perjuries
        Were gnats and flies;
It rained about him blood and tears; but he
        Drank them as free.

The fearful miser on a heap of rust
Sat pining all his life there, did scarce trust
    His own hands with the dust;
Yet would not place one piece above, but lives
    In fear of thieves.
Thousands there were as frantic as himself,
    And hugged each one his pelf:
The downright epicure placed heaven in sense,
    And scorned pretense;
While others, slipped into a wide excess,
    Said little less;
The weaker sort slight trivial wares enslave,
    Who think them brave;
And poor despiséd truth sat counting by
    Their victory.
Yet some, who all this while did weep and sing,
And sing and weep, soared up into the ring;
    But most would use no wing.
"O fools," said I, "thus to prefer dark night
    Before true light!
To live in grots and caves, and hate the day
    Because it shows the way,
The way which from this dead and dark abode
    Leads up to God,
A way where you might tread the sun and be
    More bright than he."
But, as I did their madness so discuss,
    One whispered thus:
"This ring the bridegroom did for none provide
    But for His bride."

HENRY VAUGHAN

LEAVE ME, O LOVE

Leave me, O Love, which reaches but to dust,
And thou, my mind, aspire to higher things.
Grow rich in that which never taketh rust:
Whatever fades but fading pleasure brings.
Draw in thy beams, and humble all thy might
To that sweet yoke where lasting freedoms be;
Which breaks the clouds and opens forth the light
That doth both shine and give us sight to see.
O take fast hold! let that light be thy guide
In this small course which birth draws out to death,
And think how evil becometh him to slide
Who seeketh Heaven and comes of heavenly breath.
    Then farewell, world! Thy uttermost I see:
    Eternal Love, maintain thy life in me!

SIR PHILIP SIDNEY

FORGIVENESS

My heart was heavy, for its trust had been
Abused, its kindness answered with foul wrong;
So, turning gloomily from my fellow-men,
One summer Sabbath day I strolled among
The green mounds of the village burial-place;
Where, pondering how all human love and hate
Find one sad level; and how, soon or late,
Wronged and wrongdoer, each with meekened face,
And cold hands folded over a still heart,
Pass the green threshold of our common grave,
Whither all footsteps tend, whence none depart,
Awed for myself, and pitying my race,
Our common sorrow, like a mighty wave,
Swept all my pride away, and trembling I forgave!

JOHN GREENLEAF WHITTIER

IT FORTIFIES MY SOUL TO KNOW

It fortifies my soul to know
That, though I perish, Truth is so:
That, howsoe'er I stray and range,
Whate'er I do, Thou dost not change.
I steadier step when I recall
That, if I slip, Thou dost not fall.

ARTHUR HUGH CLOUGH

TIE THE STRINGS TO MY LIFE

Tie the Strings to my Life, My Lord,
Then, I am ready to go!
Just a look at the Horses—
Rapid! That will do!

Put me in on the firmest side—
So I shall never fall—
For we must ride to the Judgment—
And it's partly, down Hill—

But never I mind the steepest—
And never I mind the Sea—
Held fast in Everlasting Race—
By my own Choice, and Thee—

Goodbye to the Life I used to live—
And the World I used to know—
And kiss the Hills, for me, just once—
Then—I am ready to go!

EMILY DICKINSON

HOLY SONNET 10

Death, be not proud, though some have callèd thee
Mighty and dreadful, for thou art not so;
For those whom thou think'st thou dost overthrow
Die not, poor Death, nor yet canst thou kill me.
From rest and sleep, which but thy pictures be,
Much pleasure; then from thee much more must flow,
And soonest our best men with thee do go,
Rest of their bones, and soul's delivery.
Thou art slave to fate, chance, kings, and desperate men,
And dost with poison, war, and sickness dwell,
And poppy, or charms can make us sleep as well
And better than thy stroke; why swell'st thou then?
One short sleep past, we wake eternally
And death shall be no more; Death, thou shalt die.

JOHN DONNE

CROSSING THE BAR

Sunset and evening star,
   And one clear call for me!
And may there be no moaning of the bar,
   When I put out to sea,

But such a tide as moving seems asleep,
   Too full for sound and foam,
When that which drew from out the boundless deep
   Turns again home.

Twilight and evening bell
   And after that the dark!
And may there be no sadness of farewell,
   When I embark;

For though from out our bourne of Time and Place
   The flood may bear me far,
I hope to see my Pilot face to face
   When I have crossed the bar.

ALFRED, LORD TENNYSON

SEEK FLOWERS OF HEAVEN

Soar up, my soul, unto thy rest,
   cast off this loathsome load;
Long is the date of thy exile,
   too long the strict abode;
Graze not on worldly withered weed,
   it fitteth not thy taste;
The flowers of everlasting spring
   do grow for thy repaste.
Their leaves are stain'd in beauty's dye
   and blazed with their beams,
Their stalks inamel'd with delight
   and limm'd with glorious gleams;
Life-giving juice of living love
   their sug'red veins doth fill,
And wat'red with everlasting showers
   they nectared drops distill.
These flowers do spring from fertile soil,
   though from unmanur'd field;
Most glittering gold in lieu of glebe
   these fragrant flowers do yield,
Whose sovereign scent, surpassing sense,
   so ravisheth the mind
That worldly weeds needs must be loath
   that can these flowers find.

ROBERT SOUTHWELL

NO COWARD SOUL IS MINE

No coward soul is mine,
No trembler in the world's storm-troubled sphere;
    I see Heaven's glories shine,
And Faith shines equal, arming me from fear.

O God within my breast,
Almighty, ever-present Deity!
    Life—that in me has rest,
As I—undying Life—have power in Thee!

Vain are the thousand creeds
That move men's hearts: unutterably vain;
    Worthless as wither'd weeds,
Or idlest froth amid the boundless main,

To waken doubt in one
Holding so fast by thine infinity;
    So surely anchored on
The steadfast rock of immortality.

With wide-embracing love
Thy spirit animates eternal years,
    Pervades and broods above,
Changes, sustains, dissolves, creates, and rears.

Though earth and man were gone,
And suns and universes ceased to be,
    And Thou wert left alone,
Every existence would exist in Thee.

There is not room for Death,
Nor atom that his might could render void:
    Thou—THOU art Being and Breath
And what Thou art may never be destroyed.

EMILY BRONTË

PROSPICE

Fear death?—to feel the fog in my throat,
    The mist in my face,
When the snows begin, and the blasts denote
    I am nearing the place,
The power of the night, the press of the storm,
    The post of the foe;
Where he stands, the Arch Fear in a visible form,
    Yet the strong man must go:
For the journey is done and the summit attained,
    And the barriers fall,
Though a battle's to fight ere the guerdon be gained,
    The reward of it all.
I was ever a fighter, so—one fight more,
    The best and the last!
I would hate that death bandaged my eyes, and forbore,
    And bade me creep past.
No! let me taste the whole of it, fare like my peers
    The heroes of old,
Bear the brunt, in a minute pay glad life's arrears
    Of pain, darkness, and cold.
For sudden the worst turns the best to the brave,
    The black minute's at end,
And the elements' rage, the fiend-voices that rave,
    Shall dwindle, shall blend,
Shall change, shall become first a peace out of pain,
    Then a light, then thy breast,
O thou soul of my soul! I shall clasp thee again,
    And with God be the rest!

ROBERT BROWNING

RESURGAM

I shall say, Lord, "Is it music, is it morning,
Song that is fresh as sunrise, light that sings?"
When on some hill there breaks the immortal warning
Of half-forgotten springs.

I shall say, Lord, "I have loved you, not another,
Heard in all quiet your footsteps on my road,
Felt your strong shoulder near me, O my brother,
Lightening the load."

I shall say, Lord, "I remembered, working, sleeping,
One face I looked for, one denied and dear.
Now that you come my eyes are blind with weeping,
But you will kiss them clear."

I shall say, Lord, "Touch my lips, and so unseal them;
I have learned silence since I lived and died."
I shall say, Lord, "Lift my hands, and so reveal them,
Full, satisfied."

I shall say, Lord, "We will laugh again to-morrow,
Now we'll be still a little, friend with friend.
Death was the gate and the long way was sorrow.
Love is the end."

MARJORIE PICKTHALL

JERUSALEM, MY HAPPY HOME

Jerusalem, my happy home,
When shall I come to thee?
When shall my sorrows have an end,
Thy joys when shall I see?

O happy harbor of the saints,
O sweet and pleasant soil,
In thee no sorrow may be found,
No grief, no care, no toil.

There lust and lucre cannot dwell,
There envy bears no sway;
There is no hunger, heat, nor cold,
But pleasure every way.

Thy walls are made of precious
        stones,
Thy bulwarks diamonds square;
Thy gates are of right orient pearl,
Exceeding rich and rare.

Thy turrets and thy pinnacles
With carbuncles do shine;
Thy very streets are paved with gold,
Surpassing clear and fine.

Ah, my sweet home, Jerusalem,
Would God I were in thee!
Would God my woes were at an end,
Thy joys that I might see!

The gardens and thy gallant walks
Continually are green;
There grows such sweet and pleasant
        flowers
As nowhere else are seen.

Quite through the streets, with silver
        sound,
The flood of life doth flow;
Upon whose banks on every side
The wood of life doth grow.

There trees forevermore bear fruit,
And evermore do spring;
There evermore the angels sit,
And evermore do sing.

Our Lady sings Magnificat
With tune surpassing sweet;
And all the virgins bear their part,
Sitting about her feet.

Jerusalem, my happy home,
Would God I were in thee!
Would God my woes were at an end,
Thy joys that I might see!

ANONYMOUS

Index